I started writing poetry when I was in school. In Elementary School much of my poetry was just for fun. In English class in High School I took writing more seriously and wanted to do some writing that people could appreciate. Most of those early attempts at poetry ended up lost and long forgotten which is probably good.

Quite a few years ago I wrote a poem on behalf of the elderly and to my surprise found it printed in the Pentecostal Testimony magazine. Several friends and relatives began asking me to write poems to honour friends or relatives which I referred to as "my odes". Then our friends, George and Vera Tyler, moved to Borneo for several years. I would write poems and email them to the Tylers to try to encourage them. They said that the poems often kept them going when things were getting difficult. Vera has for years encouraged me to publish my poems in book. When I talked to my friend, George Lewis. he urged me to publish my poems. My wife, Elvia, has also encouraged me to do so, as have our pastors, Alfred and Amie Lee. The book's name came from Elvia and our daughter, Cindy Statham who has two of her poems at the end of this book.

My theme for this volume of poems is Observations from Life. Thanks to all who encouraged me and I hope these will be a blessing to all.

CONTENTS

ANIMALS AND OTHER CREATURES

A Man And His Dog

"I love you'" the master said.

The dog looked up with loving eyes.

The master patted his soft head.

The love one only could surmise.

"The dog's a man's best friend'"

Is how the saying goes.

This friendship that will never end

Is one that everybody knows.

"Come here to me tonight",

The man calls to his scruffy dog.

The dog's eyes sparkle with delight

As to his master he does jog.

The dog's long hair he does caress.

The dog's tail wags with all his might.

The master laughs with happiness.

This love display is quite a sight.

If man and dog has love that's right,

Why can't we to folks do the same?

Each one has value in God's sight,

Regardless of his race or name.

Bug Smudge

A hundred lives or more today

Were snuffed out in a flash,

Displayed in view for all to see,

Squashed up above my dash.

The insects hit the windshield hard.

Now they'll not see the sun.

I saw them as annoying spots,

Without a care for one.

I wonder, "Do the insects scream

Before they meet their end?"

"Do they feel fear before the truck

Their little bodies rend?"

Now please do not misunderstand.

No bug grief do I share.

When cleaning insects off the glass

I find it hard to care.

A bug's life may be precious

To the bug who owns that life,

But not to one who scrapes it off

By squeegee, brush or knife.

But human life is not the same

Because each has a soul

That our Lord Jesus died to save

So that we might be whole.

An insect's life will come and go,

But we, upon this sod,

Will live to face eternity.

We must get right with God.

'GATORS

or

WHEN THINGS GET IN THE WAY

"The job is clear," the boss had said,

"The swamp , it must be drained;

So get your gear and do it now,

For you have been well trained."

I grabbed the hoses, tools and pump

And went to look around

To soon assess the best way there

To claim some higher ground.

I viewed the swamp

And saw the creek that trickled from the site;

But what I saw next stopped my breath

And caused a terrible fright.

For all across that murky swamp

Came creatures into view.

Yes, lifting up their bony heads

Were 'gators not a few.

The boss came down at evening time

To see what had been done.

The swamp should soon be empty

At setting of the sun.

The boss's expectation,

He found had not been met.

He yelled in obvious anger,

"Why is that swamp here yet?"

I said, while looking him in the eye,

Standing where those creatures romp,

"When you're up to your waist in 'gators

Who thinks of draining the swamp?"

Roadkills

God sees each sparrow when it falls.

His tender view it reaches.

That God loves every living thing

Is what this saying teaches.

Since that is true I know that God

Sees on the many highways

Each gopher, squirrel and flattened toad

By cars hit on these byways.

I've seen a hawk, a mallard too,

And even a dead 'possum,

Along with coyotes, bears and deer

And fallen moose so awesome.

I once drove through a swarm of bees

Which struck hard with a splatter.

To clean these corpses from the truck

Was quite a messy matter.

At times the death rate does increase

With seasons' warmer weather,

As insects fly across the roads

From flowers, weeds and heather.

The insects by the multitudes

Are squashed by traffic speeding.

They lose their lives and God observes

As danger they're not heeding.

Now God says you are valuable;

Much more than many sparrows.

He values humans, every one,

From modern folks to pharaohs.

That's why the Lord became a man,

With us identifying,

So He might cleanse and bring us life

By on a rough cross dying.

He loves you, friend, and sees your heart.

He knows your every sorrow.

Turn to the Lord with all your heart.

He'll give hope for tomorrow.

When you see roadkills on the way,

Remember God is caring.

No matter how things are in life

God cares how you are faring.

THE COCOON CONCEPT

Life had become difficult;

No, nigh unto impossible,

Or so I thought.

So much seems trivial

When you've been broken, chewed up and spit out.

You lie abandoned on the shelf.

You question, "Why?"

No answer comes.

You try not to get bitter.

It is a choice, you know.

So you get angry.

No, not angry, downright mad.

It doesn't help.

Who cares anyway?

You just lie shattered on the shelf.

Overlooked,

Forgotten, reputation vandalized,

Ministry gone,

Now at the bottom,

Wrapped tightly in immobilizing circumstances.

There is no way out.

That was where I was.

Then God spoke,

Not in an audible voice;

More like a strong impression.

"Remember the moth"

He was a worm once,

Just a caterpillar.

He got wrapped up in circumstances.

We call it a cocoon.

He couldn't move.

He waited a long time.

Who could know the change

That was going on inside the cocoon?

Then one day it happened. He emerged;

No longer an ugly worm,

But an elegant moth.

It would take awhile to adjust.

He did.

He lifted up on beautiful gossamer wings.

That is you in your cocoon.

You will have to wait

For a long time it seems

You will emerge;

But you will be very different.

You will rise on wings.

You will be glorious."

Some people want to break open the cocoon.

Don't!

The caterpillar will be damaged; It may even die.

Just wait.

The time will come for you.

It won't be easy. It's hard to wait,

But it will happen.

Probably when you least expect it.

Trust.

Wait.

Anticipate.

A change awaits.

A beautiful day is coming.

THE MONKEY

A monkey sat up in the tree.

I looked at him. He looked at me.

I thought, "He's cute as cute can be.

I wonder what He thinks of me.

We have a similarity

Is there a common ancestry?"

Darwin thought that he could see

That it was plain as it could be.

The monkey thought, "How can that be?

I trust God in simplicity.

Because I know that He made me,

I swing up here, a monkey free.

I don't go on a shooting spree

And kill my kin folk with great glee.

I don't drink booze 'til I can't see

And find myself out of my tree.

I don't have idiocity

Like man with his hypocrisy.

God's plan I do accept for me,

But man denies his destiny.

You think, ' A common ancestry?'

Well I'll tell you, 'I don't agree'.

I'm not from you. You're not from me.

Blame someone else but don't blame me.

CHRISTMAS

A KING SIZE BED

This king size bed was not a Tempurpedic,

A Seally, Simmons nor a Posturpedic.

It was not made of coil springs and frame.

No memory foam could this bed claim.

No bright duvet nor sheets covered this bed.

No fluffy pillows were placed at its head.

This king size bed was not like ones we own.

It was a simple one, likely of carved stone.

A mattress was not on the bed on that day.

The only softness there came from

dried hay.

This bed was used to place a

newborn stranger,

Because this king size bed was just

a manger.

You ask, "Why would you call 'king size' this small thing?"

Because this manger cradled a new young king.

"Should He not grace a crib of gold and rich blue,

If to mankind He came from heaven is true?"

He sought no privilege for Him above another,

So in this bed was placed by His dear mother.

From Jesus' birth 'til His time came to die

"He had it better," none could say, "than I."

Yes, this bed was just right for Him on that day,

Although it was so rustic, holding just hay.

Some day before this King, whose bed was small,

All will call Him " King of kings and Lord of all."

Caring For The Flock

There we were on the hillside taking care of our sheep
that night.
I thought about these animals and they just aren't too bright.
They wander off if left alone and do things that aren't smart,
But if you care for them for long they get into your heart.

Some of these sheep won't last too long past the day that
they were born;
Some we will roast or sacrifice, but the lucky will be shorn.
We'll take the wool from off their backs and they'll continue on
Enjoying slumber that is sweet until they face the dawn.

These sheep don't care what we are like as long as they
are fed.
They don't regard the slurs and nasty things that others said.
Most people think of us as rogues and worse than other men,
Just dirty shepherds watching sheep on hills or in the glen.

Our nation's founders, I recall, kept sheep and goat and cow,

As noble shepherds in their day but we are all scorned now.

To make things worse with freedom lost, with Romans we

must cope,

Despised by man and under fear we really have no hope.

We found the night wind very cold and stars were

twinkling bright.

An angel from the Lord appeared and filled our hearts

with fright.

A brilliant light surrounded us as no man ever made.

Then this big angel calmed us down with, "Do not be afraid".

"Afraid?" I thought, for there it seemed that judgment then

might fall.

He said, "I bring you tidings of great joy which is for all".

In Bethlehem a Saviour, he said, came to us that day;

We would find Him wrapped in cloths in a manger on the hay.

He said our Messiah was that Babe who also was the Lord.

An angel host came to us suddenly and said this word:

"Glory to God in the highest and peace... goodwill to men".

Then praising God the angel host returned back into heaven.

Excited we all left the sheep to find the Baby small.

Our sheep we left within the care of the Shepherd of us all.

We ran to Bethlehem and found the Babe just as we should;

Then marvelling at this great thing told everyone we could.

This little One grew up to be our Shepherd of the sheep,

And if we give our lives to Him our souls He'll surely keep.

God chose the worst and poorest men to show His grace

to all

So let us follow Him today and daily on Him call.

THE CHRISTMAS PLAN

From the glories of heaven our Father

Looked down on this earth far below

And His heart was filled with compassion

For a world full of heartache and woe.

Mankind was in need of a saviour.

They were trapped in the bondage of sin.

No-one here could bring them forgiveness

To cleanse them and place peace within.

Before time had had a beginning

The Lord God created a plan

To activate when all was ready

To reach down and rescue lost man.

All angels in heaven went silent.

An announcement would come, it was clear.

The unveiling of purpose in God's plan

Was obviously very near.

The angels all gasped in amazement

As the Father unfolded His plan;

For in bringing salvation to people

God Himself would be born as a man.

Amazement then turned into horror.

The details they could not believe.

Not born in a palace? To suffer?

What plan did the Father conceive?

In heav'n God's Son quickly stepped forth

To follow the Father's great plan;

By God's power Mary, a virigin, conceived

And the Son of God then became man.

An embryo, a fetus, a baby,

Developing in Mary's womb;

To live, then to die on a rough Roman cross,

But to rise and leave empty the tomb.

An angel choir told of His coming,

Yet not to some leader thought great,

But to shepherds out on the cold hillside,

Despised and of poor, low estate.

No royalty came to this Child.

No praises to Him did they bring,

But pagan astrologers from far, far away

In rev'rence bowed down to this King.

Some day this King will be returning,

But not as a baby that day.

Instead, He will come as the great Lord of lords

To take all His own far away.

When Christmas comes, please don't forget this:

That God came to earth as a man

And to receive love and forgiveness

You, too, must step into His plan.

Christmas Without Jesus

Christmas without Jesus

Means "Christmas" without "Christ".

The "mas" becomes a foolish "mess"

No matter how it's sliced.

The tree that points to heaven,

With shining star on top,

Becomes a silly custom

Tree huggers ought to stop.

Gift-giving has no meaning,

So selfishness then rules.

The wise men who sought Jesus

Become a band of fools.

The sparkling decorations

Lose their reason to exist;

Only sold by each store owner

To put money in his fist.

Even Santa Claus is ended.

He came from a faithful saint

Who revered the Christ of Christmas,

Showing love without complaint.

But King Jesus is the reason

For the joy that is expressed.

He came as a little baby

So the whole world could be blessed.

Christmas says there's a Saviour,

Come to give His life for all,

Resurrected, now in heaven.

Won't you now on Jesus call?

Ordinary People

It was a cool plain ordinary night;

The darkness pierced by ordinary starlight.

Across the hills lay ordinary sheep,

As drowsy shepherds fought off shades of sleep.

These folks, unknown by greats on Royal Street,

Sat quietly together with cool grass their seat.

Their genders are unknown and each one's name

Is unrecorded in a noted hall of fame.

Yet God would choose this ordinary night,

To bring God's greatest gift to man to light.

A mighty host of angels came to earth,

Declaring to these ordinary folks their Saviour's birth.

The shepherds to a simple manger came.

Some animals had eaten from the same.

A baby boy wrapped up in bands of cloth

Lay in this ordinary rough-hewn feeding trough.

Was first to theologians His birth told,

They would have wasted time out in the cold

Debating if this really could be right,

And so would miss the Saviour's birth that night.

If to King Herod Jesus' birth was shared,

He would have quickly moved, with nothing spared,

To rid himself of this threat thought his own

Of this young King whom he thought would take his throne.

God used just ordinary folks on earth

To help declare the news of His Son's birth.

His plans on earth He does fulfill, it's true

By using ordinary people just like me and you.

CHURCH MATTERS

A Church Reconciled

The time had come to reconcile.

Too few were left to walk the floors.

Too many people left in sorrow.

Wounded, they'd slipped out the doors.

Too many cutting words were spoken.

Too many friendships were destroyed.

Too many hearts were pained and bitter.

Too many souls were drained and void.

The church had now come to this crisis.

The empty pews were not a few.

If things would change to become better

One thing there was that they must do.

The corporate sins had brought destruction.

Now corporately they must turn back.

They earnestly must seek repentance

And ask the Lord to fill their lack.

To reconcile with all offended;

To make things right with those they hurt;

To offer and receive forgiveness

They must all publicly assert.

The pastor, board and congregation

Then planned a time to reconcile,

Inviting all whom they could contact,

Those gone soon or quite awhile.

The morning came to hold the service.

The sanctuary held a crowd.

Two thirds were visitors attending.

In quietness no-one seemed proud.

Prayers for forgiveness soon were spoken

For pastors and for each church board,

And for the school and congregation,

Seeking mercy from the Lord.

Some chains that held men bound were broken.

Some walls, dividing folks, came down,

The spirits bringing ill defeated,

So now this church could bless the town.

The prayers were followed by a session

Where privately they could break bread.

Tears flowed as people sought forgiveness.

They reconciled as Jesus said.

God tells us all, "Be reconciled",

So from the heart we must forgive.

Then to the world we take the message,

"Be reconciled so you can live."

A Hurting Pastor

Lord, why have I been torn out

And placed upon the shelf?

I've tried to always serve You well

And not to please myself.

What have I done that is so bad

That I face such disgrace?

If I just knew the wrong I'd done

This truth I'd gladly face.

I know I'm far from perfect, Lord,

And wrong things I have said,

But none of those deserved the guilt

Thrown down upon my head.

My reputation's ruined now,

As far as I can see.

That character remains intact

Means little now to me.

When but a boy I heard Your call.

It still burns in my heart,

But I've been thrown to the side;

In ministry no part.

I ask You to defend me, Lord.

My own words hollow ring.

No-one seems to believe me now

When I say anything.

I'm feeling torn and empty, Lord.

I sometimes feel afraid.

My future's so uncertain now.

Oh, please come to my aid.

I know that I'm not worthy, God,

But I cling to your grace

To make things right in order that

The future I might face.

You saw those called my friends attack

With hatred and deceit.

Forgetting all the love I'd shown

They stomped me with their feet.

Please help me to forgive them all

And them forgive me too,

So we can live in Your own love

As Jesus said to do.

I give it all into Your hands.

There's nothing I can do;

So work for me and make a way

And I will trust in You.

Give Your Head a Shake

(A plea to ministries' top leadership)

Give your head a shake, friend,

For times are kind of tough

And what was more than plenty once

Today is not enough.

Give your head a shake, friend.

The signs are all around.

If you don't know who's coming soon

You stand on shaky ground.

Give your head a shake, friend.

The people look to you

To give some leadership to them;

To guide and see them through.

Give your head a shake, friend.

Some pastors, bruised and torn,

Are looking for a healing balm,

Not platitudes so worn.

Give your head a shake, friend.

There's too much hurt and pain.

Don't make it worse but give a hand

To make folks whole again.

Give your head a shake, friend.

Church politics must go.

End all manipulations.

With the Holy Spirit flow.

Give your head a shake, friend.

Psychology won't do.

We're looking for a word from God

From someone just like you.

Good Church Board Members Needed

Lord, give to us elders who are led by the Spirit.

Lord, give us true deacons who know how to deac.

Lord, give us good leaders, not filled with ambition,

But servants to others, kind, humble and meek.

May they not lord over the people You've given.

May they be the ones who will follow Your will.

May they humbly seek You and follow your bidding

And even when difficult follow You still.

We need godly leaders who are an example.

We need those with wisdom, integrity, strength.

We need ones who'll do right in all circumstances

And follow the Word of God for its full length.

True leaders of God will seek God with great earnest.

True leaders of God find devotions a must.

True leaders of God will perform with compassion

While making decisions, all honest and just.

The leaders God wants will seek out what is truthful.

The leaders God wants won't be jumping the gun.

The leaders God wants will adhere to strict ethics.

They'll faithfully follow the will of God's Son.

Numbers

What is the gauge that people use

To measure church success?

The answer is quite obvious.

It's "numbers", we confess.

The leaders look for evidence

That's found in A, B, C:

Attendance, Buildings and the Cash.

It's very plain to see.

When numbers grow and cash comes in

Fine buildings we erect.

With all the best of furnishings

And finery they're decked.

We say the church that's filled with folks

Is surely a success.

The popularity we see

Could not mean any less.

However, those who fill that church

And cause the ranks to swell

Have often from small churches come.

The world speeds on to hell.

A faithful pastor of a church

In some remote small place

Cannot build up with numbers grand.

Much slower is the pace.

In one long year he gained one soul

Who had in sin been lost.

This came from many prayers and tears.

So great had been the cost!

When he went to his conference

A failure he did seem.

He could not boast, as others did,

That crowds to him did stream.

However, when he meets the Lord,

As his work finds its end,

The Lord will say, "Well done, My son,

You've been a faithful friend."

Now please do not misunderstand.

Large churches can be good.

If they lead souls to Jesus Christ

And serve God as they should.

Remember numbers aren't the gauge

Of whether things are right.

It's truth and faithfulness to God

That matters in His sight.

Removing A Pastor

The Lord does not permit you

A pastor to remove,

Unless he's had misconduct

That leadership can prove.

However, if a pastor

You'd like to move away,

There are some things to help you

To bring about that day.

First, talk about your pastor,

About how he's so good,

To churches seeking pastors

And bless them say he would.

Just minimize each weakness.

Each strong point build up high.

Find every good within him

And praise him to the sky.

Pray regularly for him

That in all he 'll succeed.

This will demand for him raise high

As this praise churches heed.

To do all this requires that

To be his friend you start.

Let him know you support him

And then hear him share his heart.

Work hard so that this vision

Becomes reality.

Then his anointed service

Will shine for all to see.

When in him you see weakness,

Then you pick up the slack.

Be strength for him in weakness

So there will be no lack.

Your pastor will get better.

His bad points will all dim.

Then other congregations

Will want to hire him.

Your goal will be accomplished,

But you'll find out in the end,

You've lost a godly pastor

And also one great friend.

THE PASTOR'S TONGUE

The pastor's tongue's a sharpened sword

That cuts and hacks at wrong,

Removing error from the flock

And guiding them along.

It also points out doctrine

That simply should not be.

Then cutting out such teachings,

It sets the people free.

It also leads to battle,

Defeating unseen foes,

Destroying principalities

The victory path it shows.

But it can be a weapon

That's used upon the sheep.

In some sad careless moment

It slashes very deep.

It too can cut at others

Also ministering grace,

Reducing reputations

To positions of disgrace.

So pastors watch your language.

Use words to guide and heal.

Don't slash at other Christians

Regardless how you feel.

With your tongue exposing error,

Cut it out as with a knife,

But when speaking of believers

Only speak forth grace and life.

The pastor's only human

So some day he'll surely fail.

Encourage, pray for him and then

He'll hear you very well.

FISHING

A Good Fishing Day

Today I'm going fishing.

I sneak from out of bed.

I want to reach the water's edge

Before the sky turns red.

Some folks say, "Why rise early?"

But it's like someone once had said,

"To early face the day is best,

For people die in bed."

I grab a hurried breakfast,

With lunch already made.

I grab my old hip waders,

In case I have to wade.

I drive to join with others.

There are more, not a few.

There's Jim, Bruce, Ethan, Jimmy,

These fishermen true blue.

We park and with our gear go,

Good fishing spots to take;

Two on a point, two by the creek

That flows into the lake.

I catch a cedar salmon,

A pine trout and spruce bass.

I even catch an alder perch

And then a clump of grass.

Then when I snag a rock cod

My line breaks with a snap.

The rod flips back toward me

And hits me with a slap.

I see the time is passing

For overhead's the sun.

I yell to my companions,

"Hey, aren't we having fun?"

My partners wave and smile.

With me they do agree.

The fishing is fantastic,

Though no fish do we see.

We break for lunch then go back.

I cast far out the lure.

As fishermen terrific,

We'll catch some fish for sure.

Time drags on by the hours.

We do not get one bite.

We've snagged more rocks and branches,

And dusk is now in sight.

I change and try fly fishing.

I cast and out it goes.

I flip it back. The hook goes wild

To catch my neighbour's nose.

Because he's angry I extract

The fly with gentle touch,

Assuring him the torn flesh

Won't really bleed that much.

The fly's name I then smile at.

Is Doc. Spratley, (that's real),

When coming out of this guy's nose

His wound he might help heal.

This fellow isn't grateful.

He belts me in the eye.

In pain I stumble backwards.

It hurts enough to cry.

No mind, I go back fishing.

My neighbour leaves the scene,

So he would not stand in my way

Where my fly could have been.

Regardless of my skillfulness.

No matter how I wish,

The sun sets low and ends my day

Without a single fish.

Then Jim pulls in a rainbow.

Although it is quite small,

We'll all go home contented.

We've not been skunked at all.

We all pack up our tackle.

To our trucks make our way.

We get the lantern and the stove,

For food at end of day.

We feast on outdoor cooking.

Camp coffee is so grand,

Although the coffee grains and ash

We spit out on the sand.

We lost some lures and sinkers.

We lost some floats and line,

But we found joy in fishing,

So everything is fine.

We all return quite happy.

When all's been said and done,

In spite of one black hurting eye

Each one of us had fun.

The Fisherman

A fisherman picked up his rods, his reels, his lures, his creel.

He went to where his boat was moored. How good it made

him feel.

He spied a youngster on the shore as he stepped on

the dock.

He smiled at that poor little guy there standing on a rock.

The little boy had not a rod. Instead he had a pole

That he cut from some bush, no doubt, the poor

misguided soul.

"Perhaps some day," the proud man thought, "That wretched

boy might too

Have proper gear and fishing boat and do as I now do."

The fisherman stood in his boat. Then he prepared to leave,

As soon as he was joined by His companions, Joe and Steve.

His friends arrived, and laughing, at the boy a glance

they gave.

He smiled from the rocky shore responding with a wave.

The fishermen untied the boat and quickly sped away.

The boy was left back on the shore to fish alone that day.

Out on the lake those fishermen tried every lure they had.

They even tried fly fishing too, but all their luck was bad.

No matter what those three men tried and cast with all

their might,

The day grew long and dusk arrived without a single bite.

They sadly put their gear away and headed for the dock.

When they arrived the boy, they found, was not upon

the rock.

Joe said, " I guess the kid was skunked and left and felt

quite blue."

An old man on the dock replied that this was just not true.

"The little boy," the old man said, "Caught lots of fish today."

"He soon filled up his limit so he up and went away."

"The little boy with pole and string, with worms and safety pin,

Brought in the fish that he required and then left with a grin."

The fishermen felt foolish when the old man shared this news.

With all their pride and arrogance they were the ones to lose.

They spent a lot of hard earned cash and time out in the sun,

But that small boy with string and pole was the person who

had won.

So when you haven't got the cash or things that others do,

Just value all that you call "yours" and make it work for you.

INTIMATE POEMS

BEFORE MARRIAGE

A Poem of Enduring Romance

You're close to the Mona Lisa,

But far lovelier than she.

You're close to the sweetness of honey,

But far sweeter than honey can be.

You're close to the wonder of Nature,

But more wonderful, I see;

But the time I love you the most of all

Is when you're close to me.

I'd Never Fall In Love

I said I'd never fall in love.

I said that I'd be wise.

But when the right girl came along

It took me by surprise.

I fell in love. It hit me hard;

But I felt like a king.

I think she's grand and that is why

I handed her the ring.

Her eyes, like emeralds, sparkle.

She's wonderful and fine.

I won't be happy 'til her name

Changes from "Moss" to mine.

She's more than any man could want.

She's sweet, she's kind, she's true.

What more can I say to show you my love,

Than, "Elvia, I love you."

When I See You

I see you. My heart jumps.

A glow comes inside.

The love I feel for you

I just cannot hide.

It's a beauty most gracious,

With which you are decked.

You're always deserving

Of love and respect.

You encourage and guide me.

You always inspire.

You are everything ever

That I could desire.

I love and adore you

And I must express

My love and devotion.

I cannot give less.

To describe how much I love you,

I am at a loss;

For words can't express it,

Sweet Elvia Moss.

AFTER MARRIAGE

Be Mine

You've stayed beside me through the years;

Held on through thick and thin.

You've faithfully been my best friend

Through all things we've been in.

You've hung in through the trials sore

That sometimes were quite bad,

But also shared the joyful times

That made us very glad.

I took you far away from home

And comforts of the east,

Not promising an easy time,

Nor life to be a feast.

I can't say that you ne'er complained

Or never wore a frown,

But you were there to pick me up

Whenever I fell down.

I love you, Elvia, my dear.

You are the very best.

What we've gone through and where we are

We never could have guessed;

But you are mine and I am yours.

All things will turn out fine.

Because you mean the most to me,

Please be my Valentine.

My Elvia

My Elvia, I love you.

I hope you know it's true.

I often think throughout the day

Of things you say and do.

I love your eyes, like emeralds,

With just a touch of green.

Yet other times they turn real blue,

So lovely to be seen.

I've always loved your smile, dear,

Sometimes a playful grin.

It makes me wonder what you've done:

What mischief you've been in.

I love the beauty of your face,

So lovely and so fair;

More beautiful with passing time

Crowned with your well-groomed hair.

I love your hair, so soft and red,

Quite pleasing to behold;

Sometimes with hints of auburn there,

But oft' with hints of gold.

I love the way you serve and care

For folks, though not your own,

Especially the elderly

Whose weaknesses have grown.

I love you for so many things

That you do say and do,

But most of all I love you, dear,

'Cause, Elvia, you're YOU.

JUST FOR FUN

A CORNY POEM

The signs along the road do tell

At each stand there is corn for sale.

There's nothing like a cob of corn

That's freshly picked that very morn.

There's Super Sweet and Jubilee,

Peaches and Cream and Illini;

All for consumers' tables grown

From seed corn that in spring was sown.

Some say that one man earned great scorn.

They called his crop "the pirate's corn",

Because he set his price too dear,

In charging all a buck an ear.

The early corn is priced too high,

But that decreases by and by.

The price goes down as fields grow old

Awaiting autumn's winds and cold.

The moral of all this is plain:

If you would hope to make some gain

Keep prices low with quality

And treat your clients cheerfully.

A POEM

A poem is just a bunch of words
Assembled to make sense.
Sometimes they're very simple,
Or maybe thick and dense.

Most follow certain patterns.
We call the rhythm, "meter".
If all the words flow easily
It makes the reading sweeter.

Most poems we read have lines that rhyme,
But some are called, "free verse".
These poems have endings which don't rhyme
Concluding quite uniquely.

I Don't Feel Like Working Today

I don't feel like working today.

There's so much at home to be done.

If I could stay home I'd be happy.

I've too many errands to run.

I don't feel like working today.

My fishing rod's calling my name.

The lake has much fish that are rising

And catching big trout is my game.

I don't feel like working today.

I guess I'm not feeling my best.

If I would just follow my feelings,

I'd turn around, go home and rest.

I don't feel like working today.

My thoughts are all going astray.

I'd like to know why I am staying.

Oh, yes, I remember! The pay.

I Forgot My Lunch

I came to work this morning

And then I had a hunch.

I looked and I discovered

That I forgot my lunch.

So now I'm feeling hungry.

My stomach starts to growl;

I think that it's my stomach

But maybe it's my bowel.

Whatever's made for supper

I know will be just great.

I hope when I arrive at home

That supper won't be late.

I know that I've decided

Wherever I may roam,

I'll make sure that I have my lunch

And not leave it at home.

Losing Things

I lost my keys the other day.

I could not drive my truck.

I could not lock the door at home

So house-bound I was stuck.

I lost my glasses one fine day.

I knew I could not drive.

I could not even read a book.

'Twas hard to be alive.

I lost my comb. I don't know where.

My hair was such a mess.

How could I fix my curly mop?

I could not even guess.

I lost my wallet in a rush

While hurrying along.

Somebody else just scooped it up,

Although it was so wrong.

I lost my pen and pencil too.

A poem I could not write.

I looked but could not find those things.

I tried with all my might.

I lost my map to find my way.

I had no G.P.S.

I sadly had to ask for help.

This thing I must confess.

I lost my dog when on a walk;

Or did my dog lose me?

In any case my canine friend

I simply could not see.

I've lost so many things in life

And things I've left behind,

But worse far still what I might lose

Is if I'd lose my mind.

Phoneless In Seattle

I'm driving to Seattle.

At home I left the phone.

I have no C. B. radio,

So I am all alone.

It's true, if I have trouble,

Nobody can I call

To help me in my sad distress,

But I don't mind at all.

No-one can call and bug me

With some new pick-up stop.

I only have to make the trip,

Then go back to our shop.

There'll be no calls to change plans

Or any such baloney.

In fact since I don't have my phone

No-one can call me phoney.

No-one can change my schedule

And thereby make me hurry.

I'm free now from such agony

That might cause me to worry.

There is more peace and much less stress.

It does not give me sorrow.

If you must call me on the phone

You'll have to try tomorrow.

Waiting

A friend once shared a funny quote:

"It doesn't take me long to wait".

It's not so simple I do note

Or otherwise it would be great.

I'm somewhat an authority

On waiting I would like to say.

Time, I think the majority,

I use in waiting day by day.

I've waited for my children dear.

I've waited for cashier and clerk.

I've waited for right words to hear.

I've waited much when I'm at work.

You'd think with so much waiting done

A patient man I ought to be,

But such is not beneath the sun

For waiting tends to frustrate me.

It does take time to wait somewhere.

It seems to me a serious waste.

If anybody had a care

You'd think they'd act with proper haste.

Now it is hard to wait for man,

But it is worse on God to wait.

He often won't reveal his plan

But asks to trust He won't be late.

To wait on God is good we know.

His promise given to us is true.

As eagles high on wings we'll go

And strength to us He will renew.

It does not make it easy, friend

To know on wings some day we'll climb.

We still must wait until the end

And waiting always takes up time.

Where's The Caboose?

When we were children we would sing

A short railroad refrain.

The song we sang was, Little Red

Caboose Behind The Train.

Now all my life I thought 'twas true

But then before my eyes,

When waiting at a crossing site,

Appeared a great surprise.

For this caboose I did not have

To wait or even hunt,

For this caboose was not behind

But was right at the front.

Could this be an exception?

But lo, I saw it twice.

Then at another crossing site

I saw the same thing thrice.

So would you please consider

That all you've heard's not true.

To search things out to find the truth

Is what we all should do.

LESSONS FROM TREES

The Tamarack

The tamarack's a tree confused.

It can't make up its mind;

Deciduous or evergreen?

No answer can it find.

In summer it's an evergreen

With needles coloured green.

Its cone shape says it's evergreen

That's clearly to be seen.

But autumn comes;

The needles change

To orange and shades of brown,

And by the time that winter's come

They've fallen to the ground.

Sometimes I'm like the tamarack;

(At least that's how I feel)

A place for me where I belong

Just simply is not real.

Yet things for me are different,

For I can hear God's voice.

Unlike the tamarack, I know

That I must make a choice.

The tamarack has not a say.

It follows in God's plan;

But I can answer, "yes" or "no",

Because I am a man.

The Cedar Tree

I see the noble cedar.

It's pleasant just to view

And odours from the cedar tree

Are pleasant to me too.

My thoughts went to my childhood

Where many cedars grew.

I made some arrows from that wood

And made a long bow too.

My brother came and said, "Let's play

Cowboys and Indians here."

He said, "I'll be the cowboy."

He ran without a fear.

I followed him so fleet of foot.

I made a whooping sound.

I shot my brother in the back

And dropped him to the ground.

My brother wore a leather coat

So him I did not kill;

But he ran to our mother.

I got a spanking still.

She tanned my hide.

She whomped me good.

She set my fields afire.

To shoot my brother in the back

I had no more desire.

Who says that punishment severe

Does not deter a crime?

To shoot my brother once again

I'd not do any time.

My mind went back to cedar trees,

More time to see I took.

I stepped up to that great big trunk

And took a closer look.

From root to crown,

From side to side

No needles did I see.

An evergreen has needles

But none grew on that tree.

The cedar tree is different.

No needles does it bear;

But neither can you call them leaves.

They simply are not there.

We might not know the greens' real name

Or what they all might be;

But just appreciate them, friend.

They're beautiful to see.

You may think you are different.

In fact, it might be true;

But you can let the beauty

Of the Lord shine out through you.

Your differences don't make you wrong.

Look at the cedar tree.

What God ordained for you to have

Is just as it should be.

No two on earth are just the same

No matter who they be.

Appreciate our differences.

Love God's diversity.

Trees

The autumn tree stands out for show

With leaves so crisp and bright,

To tell us change has come our way

For winter's just in sight.

The winter tree stands stark and bare

In frost and snow alone.

It stands for sadness, loss and death

Until the season's gone.

The spring tree stands with bursting buds

To tell new life is here.

This speaks of resurrection life

Which comes with joy each year.

The summer tree stands tall and green

With shade from summer's sun.

This shows steadfast maturity

That's shared with everyone.

The evergreen is different, though;

Its needles stay the same,

Suggesting everlasting life,

Seen even in its name.

One tree stood on a lonely hill.

Its branches formed a cross.

Like winter's tree it represented

Sadness, death and loss.

But wait, it's also like spring's tree,

With life for us arrayed;

For Jesus' death upon that tree

Brought life for sin it paid.

It's also like the summer tree,

Mature and strong to stay.

It's power works and is complete

In human lives today.

Just like the autumn tree it shows

Change to the human race.

No longer chained by rules of law,

Mankind is saved by grace.

The cross is like the evergreen

With life continuing on.

Eternal life is ours through Christ

Because the cross has won.

Whenever now you see a tree

At any time of year,

Remember one from Calvary's hill

That brought us life so dear.

The Weeping Willow

There is a tree quite beautiful.

It's called a weeping willow.

It looks like it is crying

As the breeze its branches billow.

This tree portrays a sadness,

Though it does not shed a tear.

You'll find it does shed twigs and leaves

When lawn beneath you clear.

But that's not all this willow does

In being a real pain.

Its roots clog pipes beneath the soil

When planted near a drain.

Many people who are calm and mild

When dealing with this tree

Resort to fits of fiery rage

With words that should not be.

So thus, the weeping willow

Planted there to look upon,

In fierce and plain frustration

Is extracted from the lawn.

The weeping willow is not gone.

Some tiny roots remain.

They take some water; then they grow

To form a tree again.

Some habits bad are like that tree.

They look so good to see;

But then their evil traits appear

To plague you constantly.

Soon you will find they're rooted deep.

They've now become your foe.

It's only with great agony

You force those things to go.

So friend, be careful what you plant

Within your life so dear.

Then habits that control your life

You'll never have to fear.

PROFESSIONALS

A Doctor

A doctor: friend or enemy?

Some think it's hard to tell,

Although we know he takes an oath

To try to keep us well.

Some doctors trying hard to heal

Instead bring much more pain.

They disappoint, like summer clouds

Which fail to bring the rain.

Now what we must remember

Is that doctors, too, do fail;

But their mistakes are hard to take

When we do not get well.

Saint Luke was a physician.

The Word does clearly say;

And Jesus said the sick need one,

Not those whose health does stay.

Remember doctors only aid.

The Lord alone does heal.

All healing is divine, my friend.

His care for you is real.

The doctors we appreciate.

Their efforts we applaud.

We thank them for the work they do.

For healing we praise God.

Despised Truckers

Nobody likes truckers.

Their trucks folks despise.

At least that's what Jake said,

And he won't tell lies.

It's true some are pushy

And some are quite rude,

But each trucker I know

Seems quite a nice dude.

Most truckers are friendly.

Just give them a chance.

Yet dealing with issues

They'll take a strong stance.

You must understand them.

To turn they swing wide.

Please let them manoeuvre.

Don't cut in beside.

Each truck needs some distance

In order to brake.

To drive into this space

Is quite a mistake.

View all trucks as loaded

And treat with respect.

By keeping things moving

Your good they affect.

The truckers are needed

To make business run.

The value of truckers

You don't dare to shun.

The tailgating drivers

Make truckers quite sore.

They drive far too closely

Up to the back door.

They say that they save fuel

When they're close behind.

If that truck must stop fast

Much sorrow they'll find.

Please courtesy show when

You're near any rig,

And keep driving distance

Around each truck big.

If you see trucks driving

Kind caution please take.

When they're slowly moving

Please give them a brake.

People Who Care

(A Message To Employers)

No-one faces frustration

If he's someone who just doesn't care'

But he who's concerned about issues,

When things are wrong sorrow will share.

A bank manager, who'll remain nameless,

Hurt many without a concern.

He said that he'd never get ulcers

He'd give them and make stomachs churn.

It's obvious he was quite heartless,

Foreclosing on many a farm.

He also was quite good at lying.

Unliked, he to many caused harm.

Of one fact he seemed quite ignorant

That people who care get things done.

The people who care are quite loyal

To those who things lovingly run.

When team members sometimes get upset,

To question your choices may dare,

Remember that they just are thinking

And want things to change 'cause they care.

The people who care make things happen,

Though sensitive sometimes they'll be.

They're worth all your greatest investment;

So give them respect carefully.

The Produce Farmer

"Where do the vegetables come from?"

The mom asked her son of four.

"I know that", said the little tyke,

"They come from the grocery store."

"But where does the grocery store get them?"

The little boy's mom replied.

"I do not know", the boy cried out

With his eyes opened wide.

When his dad came home from his work

His mom this matter told.

The Dad said, "We will take a trip

And see what will unfold."

On Saturday they packed the car

And drove to one big field

Where rows and rows of veggies grew.

Much produce would it yield.

The little boy in wonderment,

Amazed from his mouth spieled,

"They must have emptied out the store

To fill this great big field."

"No", laughing, his dad said to him.

"Oh, no", said his mom too.

"The farmer grows plants in his field

Beneath the sky so blue.

"When these plants reach maturity

Before they get too old,

The farmer takes them from the ground,

Then to the store they're sold.

Out there the farmer working hard,

A hoe with skill did wield.

"No doubt, the farmer", said his dad,

"Is outstanding in his field."

The little boy a lesson learned

From looking at this land.

All food that we find in the store

Comes from a farmer's hand.

We do applaud these ones who work

So hard what e'er their mood,

And give themselves across this land

Providing us with food.

RESURRECTION

Alive?

"Alive", you say, but I heard Him cry,

"It is finished". Then I saw Him die.

They placed His body in a tomb of stone,

So cold, abandoned, so alone.

They sealed the door with the rock they rolled,

So huge 'twould halt the strong and bold.

To make sure the body none would steal,

They sealed the stone with a Roman seal.

When one was dead the Romans knew.

They had killed many, not a few.

They pierced His side with a sharpened spear

Because the Sabbath day was near.

He must be dead and moved away

So the Jews could keep that holy day.

Yes, He was dead of that they knew.

Their day was done. Their job was through.

The empty tomb says, "He's not dead."

This One is risen as He said.

No more with sins need people strive.

He paid the price. He is alive.

He Is Living!

I know! I know! I know!

No doubt can seize my mind.

The Nazarene named Jesus

Lives and left the tomb behind.

He's risen and He's living,

Interceding for His own.

He's seated with the Father,

Not held in a tomb of stone.

I know! I know He's living,

Having died upon a tree.

I know that He is living

For Christ Jesus lives in me.

He Is Risen Indeed

"He is risen, indeed!" the mocker scoffs.

His voice is filled with scorn.

His heart is hard and cold,

Yet empty and forlorn.

"He is risen, indeed?" the doubter asks.

His voice is filled with fear.

His heart fights unbelief;

No confidence is near.

"He is risen, indeed?" the seeker probes.

His voice is filled with hope.

His heart hopes for the best.

If true, then he can cope.

"He is risen, indeed!" the angel states,

With strong voice by the tomb.

The truth is obvious.

It's just an empty room.

"He is risen, indeed!" the believers cry,

Their voices with faith strong.

Their hearts rejoice in Jesus,

Filled with a victory song.

"He is risen, indeed!" we cry with joy.

The sacrifice avails.

The blood shed for mankind

Redeems and never fails.

"He is risen, indeed!" with triumph shout.

The victory has been won;

The devil, sin and death

O'ercome for everyone.

SPIRITUAL THOUGHTS

Absolutes

We used to have some absolutes,

But things have turned around.

The standards we relied upon

Are nowhere to be found.

Some say we weren't created.

We just happened, so I'm free

To make my own rules and create

My own reality.

But absolutes I know exist.

Is see them everywhere.

They rule all things in outer space,

In earth, in sea, in air.

Without the laws of science true,

An engine cannot run.

Without some absolutes in space

A space trip can't be done.

When some say, "there's no absolutes"

Is absolutely real,

This is a contradiction.

They have made one with this spiel.

No, you are not a happenstance;

Created you have been,

And your Creator has some rules

Which clearly can be seen.

Our God created absolutes

To make all things work well.

It would improve our knowledge too

If these things we would tell.

Yet absolutes are not just words,

But truths to guide our lives.

If we would follow them we'd find

The peace for which each strives.

Anyway

When in life you're successful

To bring a better day,

Though some may harshly criticize,

Then do it anyway.

When you know if you counsel

Someone to find the way,

That in return they'll trash your name,

Then do it anyway.

If you'd do good to others

But mean things some folks would say

As they misjudge your motives pure,

Then do it anyway.

If you defend another,

Unjustly hurt one day,

And this brings scorn from someone else,

Then do it anyway.

When if your love's extended

To some poor soul today,

Tomorrow you'll be chastised sore,

Then do it anyway.

If you can ease a burden,

Though this one cannot repay,

Though it may cost you something great,

Then do it anyway.

When we were lost in darkness,

With no light, no, not a ray,

To save us Jesus faced the cross.

He did it anyway.

Christian Nerds

There are some people in the church

Described by nasty words;

Like "strange", "embarrassing" and "weird".

They're known as "geeks" or "nerds".

They're pushed into the background.

Rejection brings them hurt.

The other Christians laugh at them

And treat them just like dirt.

They're told they do not properly dress.

They don't know how to talk.

They do not eat the way they should

And awkwardly they walk.

They're centred out from all the rest.

Acceptance they can't find,

But Jesus sees their lonely hearts.

He keeps them in His mind.

Not many strong, not many wise,

Not called are many great;

So Christian nerds are all okay.

With Jesus they do rate.

So Christians seek forgiveness

For the way you treat these nerds.

Remember, you're no better

If you're sinful in your words.

On earth the Christian nerds will face

Rejection and disgrace.

In heaven, I'm sure God's prepared

For them a special place.

Contentment

Paul said he'd learned to be content

Whatever be his state;

While suffering in prison chains

Or feeling very great.

Why can we not have peace, like Paul,

Whatever be our lot?

Some hopeless dreams that many have

Are those things that we've got.

Unthankful hearts control our minds.

We whimper and we whine,

While basking in our affluence,

Of things not yours or mine.

God has a plan that supersedes

All things we might desire.

His plan will bring us joy and love

But also pain and fire.

God asks for faith so we'll believe

He'll give whatever's best.

The glory that will be revealed

Comes when we pass the test.

Though you may doubt, God knows what's good;

So rest in what's for you.

Be thankful for all little things.

Then see what God will do.

Envy Not The Evil Man

Envy not the evil man who has all things today,

Who tramples roughshod o'er each one who's standing in

his way.

He pushes, shoves to gain more ground, so all will do

his will;

Then by the masses praise receives as his proud cup

they fill.

He glories in the accolades that he does not deserve,

As hosts of people, just like slaves, his selfish

pleasures serve.

He seems so blessed with everything and seems to

have it all.

Yet no-one seems to know the truth about his coming fall.

For those things that he revels in will bring

impending doom.

The judgments that are facing him on his horizon loom.

The many things that he holds dear are just a passing fad.

They'll soon be gone and great remorse will make his heart

turn sad.

He'll face the judgment for his ways with no time to repent.

All hope for mercy or reprieve he'll find already spent.

Do not begrudge him of his gains from evil ways so rife.

The only pleasure that he'll know is what's found in this life.

As he receives the recompense for his own wicked ways,

Some, who on earth he did destroy, will enter better days.

For his own wickedness he'll pay and judgment he will see,

But faithful ones will get rewards for all eternity.

Don't envy him whose ways are wrong but for him all

seems well.

Remember sadly he will face eternity in hell.

No need to envy evil men. Look to the future prize.

Know God is fair and in the end will show that He is wise.

False Hope

I've heard the "prophecies", the "words",

Encouragement meant to bring.

I've heard the great predictions

Which cause the heart to sing.

In midst of tribulations sore

For answers one will grope.

These words meant to encourage

Bring a flickering ray of hope.

Then time continues on and on.

The changes do not come.

The circumstances bringing pain

Beat on just like a drum.

The Word says when hope is deferred,

It makes the heart grow sick;

But false hope leads to deep despair.

Depression comes on thick.

So, Lord, please keep away false hopes.

I wish them to be done.

If void of hope that's genuine,

It's better to have none.

I know my hope should rest in you,

My Saviour and my God;

But faith has grown weak today

As on life's path I trod.

So, Jesus, I depend on You

To build my faith and hope.

On You alone I can depend

To help me stand and cope.

False hopes be gone forevermore.

In God I hope and trust.

This hope is real and holds me firm

For keep his Word He must.

Forgiveness And Trust

A girl, abused and beaten up,

Seeks help from anyone.

The family is embarrassed

By what the dad had done.

Officials then investigate,

Recording what they've seen,

With evidence considered,

It's time to intervene.

The dad is dealt with harshly.

They keep him out of range.

He swears and curses each one,

Intending not to change.

A counselor helps calm her
So healing soon can start.
She longs for love authentic
With all her little heart.

The counselor soon tells her
If happily she'll live,
She must put this behind her
And then her dad forgive.

Yet she can't trust her daddy.
She can forgive the wrongs,
But she can't have a pure love
From dad for which she longs.

Forgiveness does not bring trust.
To build trust takes much time.
With her dad she cannot have
A relationship sublime.

So call forgiveness, "kindness",

"compassion" if you must,

Or "reconciliation",

But don't you call it, "trust".

God's Promises

A soft voice says, "So that's how God

Rewards your faithfulness!

He sets you up, then knocks you down,

And leaves you in a mess."

"You've sacrificed and given all.

He's promised you the prize;

But now He's turned His back on you.

You can't believe such lies."

But friend, this voice that is so soft

Is not from God above.

If comes from the deceiver's lips.

He tries to hide God's love.

God's love still reaches out to you.

He holds you in His care.

Although it seems that all is lost,

God's presence still is there.

He doesn't tell the reason why

You face such grief and pain.

He only asks to trust Him more

For this will be your gain.

The promises of God above

Are true and will not fail.

He'll take you through the storms of life.

His vict'ry will prevail.

All storms on earth come to an end.

Then light comes shining through.

Our trials will also finally end

With blessings that are new.

As harvest-time comes in the fall

Our God will not be late.

He promises good things for those

Who on the Lord do wait.

So don't believe the tempter's lies.

God's promises are true.

Hold on to Christ with faithfulness.

He'll bring good things to you.

Heading Home

I've enjoyed this little visit.

My time here has been nice.

In fact things that have happened

Have really been a slice!

Some storms of life I've weathered.

To places I did roam.

It's all been fascinating,

But soon I'm heading home.

It's sometimes fun to travel

Over land and ocean's foam,

But nothing's quite as special

As to know you're headed home.

Soon my stay here will be over.

My life's goal I'll finally win.

I will make my journey homeward

To a place I've never been.

I sense great anticipation;

No desire more to roam.

With my Saviour there to meet me

I will reach my heavenly home.

HIGHS AND LOWS

When you have soared as an eagle

And felt the clouds brush past your face,

It's hard on earth once more to settle

And keep abreast life's hectic pace.

When you've walked with Christ on the water

Above all the ebb and the flow,

It's hard to climb into the boat once again

And sitting there help the crew row.

When you have stood high on a mountain

And thrilled at the sights all around,

It's hard to descend to the valley

And once more reside on low ground

Yet eagles find food in the valleys

And distance is gained by the oars.

The fruit trees don't grow on the summit.

The farmers below fill the stores.

The Lord sends us times of refreshing.

We soar as on God we do wait.

We revel in walking with Jesus.

The Spirit's touch makes us feel great.

Yet we must come down to the battle.

There's truth from God's Word we must search.

There are souls to be rescued for Jesus

And distance to gain for his church.

The trials we find in the valleys

Grow fruit in our lives every day.

Thank God for the times of refreshing,

But press on with God all the way.

I Saw A Sign

I saw a sign the other day.

It almost made me cry.

No hope was found in those sad words.

"LIFE SUCKS AND THEN YOU DIE."

I saw a sign on one short street.

Some humour did I find.

"DEAD END" was written on the sign.

A graveyard was behind.

I saw a sign which said, "THE ONE

WHO DIES WITH THE MOST TOYS WINS"

And yet no great prize was offered there.

It dealt not with our sins.

I saw a sign which gave me hope.

Its words were, "JESUS SAVES",

Not talking about money, friend,

But sins which he forgave.

I saw those signs which spoke of death

When life on earth is done.

The last, alone, gave future hope

Through Jesus Christ, God's Son.

Cold Religion Does Not Cut It On The Street

It's cold on the street tonight.

Snow swirls around in the sharp frigid wind.

My jacket tries to resist the icy fingers of the frost.

It's too thin, too worn and too old.

Something like me.

I've seen it all, had it all and done it all.

There's not much left.

No-one cares.

I don't blame them.

I have nothing to give back.

Yes, thin, worn and old

And now I'm cold, so very cold.

A lady told me of Jesus today.

She said He cared and so she cared.

I needed shelter

Or even something hot to drink.

She said she could not help me.

She cared but could not help.

Yea, right! I've heard it all before.

I tried religion once.

"Clean up, quit drugs, dress like us or get out," they told me.

I didn't fit.

I got out.

Maybe that dumpster will keep me warm.

Oh, good, it has lots of boxes;

Good insulation, you know.

Maybe I won't freeze after all

Like Ned did last night.

Took him off stiff as a board.

Well, he won't hurt anymore.

It will be very cold tonight but I'll probably make it.

Too bad I can't find some warmth for my cold, cold heart.

It's so lonely out here

And nobody cares;

But that's what it's like

On the street.

Make A Difference

It's easy in life to put people down;

To call them idiot, fool or a clown.

You don't need intelligence to show that you're rude,

To make criticism your harsh daily food.

It may be an effort to try to impress,

Or raise yourself up as you make others less.

However, such words only bring yourself low.

Your own weaknesses and your failures you show.

We need to encourage instead of put down.

We need to bring smiles instead of a frown.

We need to let love through our speaking abound,

So others will be glad that we've been around.

Love covers all failures. Love covers all sin.

Let love touch all others wherever they've been.

Let's drop all cruel mocking and build up instead.

Let's make a real difference through all that we've said.

The Potter's Wheel

The old man sat at the potter's

Wearing a happy grin.

He placed some clay on the wheel of stone

And started it to spin.

Faster and faster he turned the wheel

Until the speed was right.

With gnarled fingers he pressed the clay

With pressure firm but light.

In a little time the soft clay rose.

A shape began to form,

As fingers gently pushed and squeezed

The softened clay so warm.

Then suddenly the old man's face

Took on a darkened frown.

He'd felt some foreign substance there.

He smashed the structure down.

It wasn't that the shape was wrong.

Some dirt he felt and saw.

If he had left it in the clay

The piece would have a flaw.

When all the bits had been removed,

He spun the wheel once more.

The vessel started taking shape;

Much better than before.

The potter, finished with his work,

Then let the wheel go still.

He took the vessel in his hands

And placed it in the kiln.

Now God our heavenly potter is.

We are the potter's clay.

God works through circumstances now

To mold us every day.

Sometimes He has to smash us down,

For things that don't belong

Must be extracted from our lives

To cleanse us from all wrong.

At times the Lord may squash us down

To give us shape that's new,

So we will have a proper form

For what He's called us to.

Sometimes when we are on the wheel,

Our lives spin 'round and 'round.

We don't know what is happening

And answers can't be found.

We mustn't squirm as we are formed,

But quietly must wait.

When we are finished spinning 'round

For service we will rate.

It isn't wrong to question things

And ask the reason why;

But never doubt God's faithfulness.

He'll show you by and by.

God loves you so He'll mold you well

Into a vessel true.

Then He will fill you with His grace

To share with others too.

To be a chosen vessel means

A process hard to take,

But in the end a purpose great

Fulfilled for Jesus' sake.

MY FIRST VISION
(at age 14)

Sleeping, sleeping, sleeping,

But suddenly awake.

What is this scene before me?

Of it what can I make?

I close my eyes. I open them.

I pinch myself and see

I hurt and know it's not a dream,

But what can this thing be?

Raging, raging, raging;

A river rushes on.

Young people in its current

Sweep by and then are gone.

I see the river's final end.

A change comes to its flow;

A waterfall is plunging down

To darkness thick below.

Trembling, trembling, tremblling:

Inside I cry, "Oh, no!"

Some teens inside that river

Are people whom I know.

Some adults then start praying,

Although there's just a few.

This sets up nets that hold some firm

While others plunge from view.

Changing, changing, changing;

The scene becomes a slide.

The same ones whom I saw before

Are going for a ride.

The slide ends at a huge square hole

With sides that funnel down,

To darkness spewing tongues of fire

Just like an evil crown.

Sliding, sliding, sliding;

So many moving fast

And unaware their thrilling ride

Just simply cannot last;

But prayers rise up from faithful saints.

A trap door shuts down tight

To hide the hole and save the few

Not yet gone out of sight.

Rising, rising, rising;

Great shouts of joy and praise,

For from the river and the slide

Some souls our Lord did raise.

'Twas not because of someone great

Held up for all to see,

But just because of faithful prayers

From folks like you and me

Fading, fading, fading;

And then the vision's gone.

Its impact leaves me feeling weak.

The Spirit's work is done;

For urgency has gripped my heart.

God's people need to pray,

To intercede for all the lost

And judgment on them stay.

Praying, praying, praying;

We must! We dare not nap,

But halt them in their downward plunge

By standing in the gap.

Let's raise a barricade of love

Which they cannot go through

And then with Christ our Lord in heav'n,

One day they'll join us too.

My Tongue Got In The Way

My day has turned to sadness.

I'm feeling down today.

I meant to speak forth blessing

But my tongue got in the way.

Instead I spoke forth error.

It brought forth hurt and pain.

Instead of bringing cleansing,

My tongue produced a stain.

My tongue's a wild creature,

Not tamed, I know full well.

No wonder that the word declares

It's lit by fires of hell.

Now I must make confession

To God for what I've blurt,

And also seek forgiveness

From the one I badly hurt.

I understand king David

When to God the psalm he'd sung,

Asking God to guide each word

With a guard upon his tongue.

So Lord, fight fire with fire

To stop the evil blaze.

With Holy Spirit fire

Make my tongue watch what it says

Reconsidering Success

Once thousands followed eagerly

As with bread He did bless.

When He said things hard to explain,

Some left and there were less.

As leaders of the way of God

Said that He was not true,

More turned away, rejecting Him,

So then there were but few.

Then even closest followers

Ran off, except for four.

His mother, John and Marys two

Stood by. There were no more.

He'd plunged from greatness to defeat,

As men would gauge success.

I'm certain people wondered there

Why He was in this mess.

Rejected, mocked and beaten sore,

He hung up on the cross.

He felt forsaken by His God.

He suffered pain and loss.

As Jesus died, in heaven above

I'm sure that praises swelled.

The keys of death and hell, our sins,

Within His hands He held.

This scene was not one of defeat,

But one of victory.

The price for all sin had been paid.

Now people can be free.

They placed Him in a borrowed tomb,

But from it He did go,

Declaring triumph over all

So that the world might know.

What often looks like failure sad,

I truly now confess,

Is not defeat, but in God's plan,

Instead is great success.

Religious Fears

"Fear not!" was heard in Bible days.

These words through Scripture ring.

They're heard in Christmas dramas

As we hear the angels sing.

From Abraham, called Abram,

Old Testament saint of old,

To Cornelius, a centurion,

In Peter's day we're told.

All heard the words that they fear not

When to them angels came.

Today when God comes near in power

His words are just the same.

We ask for God to send His power

And send His awesome grace,

But then we fear and criticize

When He comes face to face.

"This can't be God", we do declare.

"This just is not God's way.

We've never seen these things before.

They can't be right today."

We ask for God to come in pow'r,

His presence to display;

Yet when He comes and things do shake

In fear we turn away.

If we ask God for heav'nly things

Which in God's Word we read,

Be sure He won't give us a stone

Or scorpion instead.

If we have faith to ask for things

We need faith to receive

And take God at His promise that

He'll give what we believe.

Religious fear is always scared

Of what God's power might bring;

But godly fear of God alone

Will make the heart to sing.

The fear of God will set us free.

It does not paralyze,

And cause us to reject things new

That in the church may rise.

Religious fear will always say,

"Those things cannot be right",

But godly fear will check to see

How they are in God's sight.

Let's not be judges that condemn

And others criticize.

As harmless as doves let us be;

As serpents let's be wise.

Relinquishment

Sometimes the things that come our way

Are not what we adore.

We cry in our frustration,

"Lord above, no more, no more!"

We wait for God to intervene

And change our earthly plight.

If God does not soon alter things

We pout, complain and fight.

We want our circumstances changed

To fit the way we're bent;

But God is waiting for our wills

To show relinquishment.

The Lord desires to change our lives

And make us like his Son;

Not all our circumstances changed

So we say we have won.

The greatest victory is the cross.

There's one that each must bear.

It leads us to the death of self.

Then Christ's life we will share.

Don't fall into depression, then,

When all your hopes grow dim.

God's testing is perfecting you

To be much more like him.

The answer is in yielding, friend,

To God in all you do.

Relinquish all to His designs

And He will see you through.

Selfishness

We all say that we want to do

The things that are for us God's will;

But often it does not prove true.

Our own ways we desire still.

We think our faithfulness does rate.

"We've put God first," we proudly say.

When closer we investigate

We often find self in the way.

Although the Bible says to love

Our neighbour as we love ourselves,

As each will try to rise above

In status he his kindness shelves.

We seek our own good and forget

Our neighbours who around us live;

Ignoring all their needs we let

Them have much less than we could give.

We say that first we have put God

And so we'll do just as He says;

But when His way seems hard to trod

We turn and go our merry ways.

We fight for self and our desires

But say the Lord we want to please.

We need to quench these selfish fires

And seek repentance on our knees.

The only right way is God's way.

No other should we seek to find.

Endeavour to serve God each day

And leave your selfishness behind.

Some Things God Cannot Do

There are some things God cannot do.

I've read His Word.   I know it's true.

God cannot sin. Such is absurd,

For God is pure. It's in His Word.

He cannot lie. A lie is sin.

Truth is the thing that God walks in.

Himself, the Lord God can't deny.

To do this thing would be a lie.

God cannot run away and hide.

He's everywhere , both far and wide.

God can't gain strength to stronger be.

He is all-powerful, you see.

To learn some thing God cannot do.

He knows all there's to know. It's true.

God can't love wrong or hate what's right.

His righteous character holds tight.

God does good only, as He must;

This Faithful One, whom we can trust.

The Narrow Way

"We mix so much with Jesus", I heard the preacher say.

This made me do some thinking about the gospel way.

Straight is the way and narrow is the gate to eternal life.

So said our Lord and Saviour above the noise and strife.

There's only one way to this life. You must be born again.

Accept the sacrifice of Christ to cleanse from sinful stain.

You cannot serve two masters. The Bible tells us so;

So put your trust in Christ alone and victory you will know.

The truth may seem restrictive; the way may seem confined,

But you cannot change God's design with thoughts from your

own mind.

We can't mix truth with error, however good it seems,

Or we'll find in eternity we based our hopes on dreams.

Don't redefine the Scriptures. Accept God's Word as true.

You'll find His way the only way and peace will come to you.

Reject the thoughts and theories that with God don't agree.

Instead draw close to Jesus, the greatest friend there'll be.

Believing is not sufficient: Demons in fear believe.

You must commit yourself to Christ and Christ

Himself receive.

The answer's not in striving, religion or such a thing;

But rather in relationship with Jesus Christ the King.

Do not mix things with Jesus for Jesus is enough,

The only Truth and only Way who helps when times

are tough.

Renew your mind with Scripture.   God's Word will show

the way

Just give your life to God's control and let Him lead each day.

The Search

I searched for love my aching loneliness to end.

The friends I found all finally let me down.

Their love depended on performance they required.

Then when I failed no love was left around.

I searched for meaning in a life frustrated.

I found philosophies and purposes so grand.

Yet when the test of time came down upon them,

They crumbled like a castle made of sand.

I searched for pleasure in a life of sorrow.

Activities I tried to bring me fun.

All fun soon vanished like the mist of morning,

Dispelled by heat from morning's rising sun.

I searched for life to make all seem worthwhile,

Yet life seemed futile, empty and so vain;

But all I tried to satisfy my longings,

Resulted only in a heart of pain.

I searched for God without expecting answers.

He came to me as Jesus Christ the Lord.

He brought me love that's real with life and purpose

And lasting pleasure through His precious Word.

All expectations that I sought I found were empty.

All good things that I wanted and me enticed

Came not from effort for the things I reached for,

But freely came through grace by Jesus Christ.

They Say I'm Old

They say I'm old,

And that my mind is slipping.

They say that all my good years are behind;

But I just smile,

For in those lonely hours

I search God's Word and daily treasures find.

They say I'm old,

My hair is white and thinning.

My memory is not quite so good, I know;

But there are things

I always will remember,

"How God's been faithful and leads me as I go."

They say I'm old,

And that my work is finished;

That things of value no longer can I do.

Yet I can pray,

Encourage, love, and witness.

I'll share a smile and cheer somebody too.

They say I'm old,

My skin is getting wrinkled.

My feet are slow and don't move as they could;

But firmly planted

Are my feet in Jesus,

So safe am I, protected by his blood.

They say I'm old,

And won't be here much longer.

My health has failed, my course will soon be run;

But I am young,

For soon I'll be with Jesus.

I will rejoice; my future's just begun.

TRIBUTES

A Baby Boy!

A baby boy! A precious gift from God!

A ray of sunshine on life's path you trod!

This little bundle represents your love

Established in your hearts from God above.

A little life for which you both must care!

A tiny one whose growing pains you'll share.

This one is yours to shelter, teach and guide;

By your example, strengthened by your side.

Instill in him God's values every day.

Then from the path of goodness he won't stray.

He'll make you laugh and sometimes make you cry.

His time with you will sometimes bring a sigh.

172

He'll let you down and sometimes drive you wild,

But just remember he's your precious child.

At all times give him gentleness and care.

Consistency will teach him you are fair.

He is so very small, so very weak.

He is too young to share his thoughts and speak,

But still you are a boy with noble names.

We welcome to this family you, Roy James.

by Grandpa Hubbeard

A Boy Is Born

The Edmonton sky was sunny and bright

O'er Royal Alexandra Hospital that day.

A love gift, so precious, from God up above

To the Statham home came then to stay.

On October 17, 2004,

With Grandma Sharon and Bruce by her side.

Cindy gave birth to a bright little boy

And brought happiness no-one could hide.

They called his name Ethan, then William, then Ronald,

A long name for a fellow only 20 inches long;

But Poppa called him "Tiger" and who was surprised

When Nanny created for him a new song.

Only 6.9 pounds, this cute little fellow

Looking much like his daddy, there bursting with pride,

Brought joy to the family and friends all around

And who could their love and excitement then hide?

The given name, Ronald, was special, you see,

Named after his own Poppa's identical twin,

Who'd pastored and ministered over the years,

But then slowly succumbed as cruel cancer did win.

This bright little fellow so strong, full of life,

We pray that the Lord will forever watch o'er.

As he grows through various stages of life

May he faithfully walk with the Lord evermore!

by Poppa

A Baby Girl!

Another precious gift from God,

Come to us from above.

This special little baby girl

Arrived to share your love.

This little girl, all bundled up,

With such a charming smile

Stole each one's heart and brought them joy

To last for quite awhile.

A little life to teach and guide

And show her loving care!

Her progress and her failures both

Are things you too will share.

Instill in her the truths of God

And values every day.

Then she will know which way to go

On life's tempestuous way.

She'll make you cry. She'll make you laugh.

She'll drive her brother wild.

But just remember who she is,

Your precious loving child.

Anticipation filled us up

Before she came our way,

So eagerly we welcome her,

Our own Hallie Monet.

by Grandpa Hubbeard

A Baby Girl Is Born

It was a snowy March 10th , 2006,

Royal Alexandra Hospital, the place!

In the room with Cindy were Sharon and Bruce

And outside Grandpa Erv, who did pace.

At exactly twenty minutes past eleven that morn,

The Statham's received a new girl;

Elvia Natasha Sharon, her name,

A gift much more precious than pearl.

And so it was poppa, in a place far away,

Rejoiced and called this one his "jewel".

So cherished and priceless this gift from the Lord

Warmed their hearts 'though outside it was cool.

They say she came home through a snowstorm so wild,

All bundled up warm as could be.

To share as a Statham, the love that is found

In each one of the whole family.

It did not take long 'til a song was prepared

By her Nanny who sang it by phone.

It soon was apparent with so much love shown

She never need feel she's alone.

But greater than this is God's love for this girl

Who showers it on her each day.

We pray that she always will cherish His love

And always will walk in His way.

by Poppa

A Birthday Poem for Janet Hazel Clark

When my twin and I were born premature,

We were put in an incubator,

So we had to wait to meet all of our kin.

In fact, it would be a lot later.

When we did come home, we wowed one of the girls,

Who stared like we were from a strange planet.

That this was our sister we learned later on

And she would be known as "Janet".

Over eight years before, this sister was born

And "Janet Hazel" was given her name.

The large number of the Hubbeard brood she did increase.

To a total of nine was her game.

She was going to school as I grew as a child

So she spent much time studying hard.

For most of the time she was hitting the books

I was playing with friends in the yard.

As I neared my teen years both parents were talking

Of something to which we should hark.

This sister of mine was dating, was engaged

And married a man, "Ivan Clark".

Many hours I have spent as the years hastened by

With this couple and oh, it was grand.

As we discussed cars and important world news

Janet kept lots of coffee on hand.

Well, this couple increased as some children were born

From the number of two up to six.

With Debbie and Joannie and Marion and Rob

To Cavan they moved from the sticks.

Life sometimes was hard for this mother of four

With surgeries, sickness and fear,

But Janet was not one to quickly give up

So she'd press on and persevere.

With grand children and great grand children as well

She has family members around.

With siblings and nephews and nieces as well

To her lots of love does abound.

They say that the cream always goes to the top

And with Janet we found this is true.

She rose to the top and is loved by us all.

Now seventy she has reached too.

Hat's off to my sister who's made it this far.

May she celebrate and be real glad;

And may the next seventy years that she has

Be the best years that she's ever had.

Tribute To Audrey Hynson

It all began some years ago when Elvia and I

Met someone named Maria who was anything but shy.

While helping with her mission, soon her daughter we

did meet.

Then Audrey introduced us to her family so sweet.

Spending much time with these folks, our care for

them grew

Now we feel so close that we are almost family too.

We spent much time with Audrey, with her mother and

with Gord.

We'd eat together, work or pray and talk about our Lord.

When we talked about spiritual gifts, she asked what hers

could be.

I said, "You are a server. It is very plain to see."

She cared a lot for people and to help she felt

she should.

She'd cook and bake for hours, helping all of those that

she could.

She often shared some time with us; some times were

good, some sad.

She would move forward through it all and in time we

were glad.

I'll not forget the glad day when Leona and Stephen wed.

"If they're not here soon, we will start without those two",

she said.

Returning from the USA with goods that she there got,

To others she would often share the things that she

had bought.

We trust she's looking down at us from up in

heaven above;

This lady who is precious in our memory with love.

A Tribute To Marjorie

I praise my sister, Marjorie,

Who, until I was age ten,

Because our births were far apart,

Seemed like my aunt 'til then.

On April 14, '27,

To Hubbeard's home she came;

The first of seven little girls,

Marjorie Elizabeth by name.

She always was a worker;

Hard work ever seemed her fare;

For even as a little girl

For her sisters she would care.

Her older brother, Norman,

Chopped some wood, so it is said.

She ran between the axe and block.

He cut her skull instead.

She was quite young. Her wound bled,

But she survived quite fine.

She'd stay well back when anyone

Was chopping wood next time.

For people called "the Howards"

In housekeeping she would work.

In Payne's Dry Goods Store as a clerk

From hard work she'd not shirk.

She met and married Thomas Pinck

In 1947.

The next year Marjorie had a boy,

Young Alan, a gift from heaven.

Then Barbara, their first girl was born,

A red-head girl so dear.

Then Wendy came, the second girl,

To bring their family cheer.

The first years of her married life

Was near Millbrook, Ontario;

Then to the army base out west

In B.C. they did go.

Near Vedder Crossing was their base,

At Cultus Lake, their home.

From family they seemed far away;

Such distance did they roam.

A cousin, named Jean Caldwell,

Asked her to her church. She came.

'Twas there she gave her life to Christ.

She never was the same.

Then they moved back to Millbrook.

Near the town they chose to dwell.

Sadly, there her little Barbara

Died when falling down the well.

For Doc Hobbs she was working,

Cleaning, sometimes on her knees.

She declined when once he offered

Chocolate-covered ants or bees.

She learned to play the violin.

She played piano too.

The violin was Norman's

And his use for it was through.

They then adopted children:

Ruth and Danny, as was mete,

Then Patricia, Kevin, Andy

Made the family complete.

They bought a farm on Zion Line.

A garden they did grow.

With pickles, vegetables and jams

To market she would go.

When Tommy found Christ Jesus,

Marjorie's life would better be.

The change was clear when they would come

To visit Elvia and me.

They sold the farm on Zion Line.

In Cardiff they would stay.

We helped them pack and move their goods

And they went on their way.

They oft' would go to Florida

To find a warmer day.

One spring while driving homeward

Marjorie's Tommy passed away.

Then Marjorie moved from Cardiff

To a trailer park in Keene.

While at the church in Millbrook

She met Albert Witteveen.

In time the two were married.

A better match there could not be,

For he always loved and helped her

And so happy she would be.

My sister was a trooper,

Staying true to all she knew;

So, you I honour, Marjorie,

For all the things that you've gone through.

An Ode to Beatrice Hubbeard

From Montreal city a young woman came,

And Miss. Beatrice Dawson was this lady's name.

To a local Bible college this Beatrice did go,

Called "E.P.B.C." in Peterborough.

One time in the fall of 1953

The church in Millbrook she desired to see.

Along with the pastor, Fred and Betty Spring,

She started a new path with her country fling.

Then the Hubbeard family thought that it was fine

To ask that the three of them would come to dine.

She seemed to feel comfortable out at the farm.

The countryside seemed to hold to her some charm.

With her studies in Bible College complete

She thought she'd move to a place on Water Street.

She wanted a roommate and thought that she should,

So she shared the apartment with friend, Betty Good.

She soon made a choice that she thought was the wiser,

So she bought a green car that had a sun visor.

She's one who'd accomplish whenever she'd strive,

So at the farm Jean helped her learn how to drive.

She worked for many years at C.G..E.

Then did home care a while with glee.

She had as her friends children, animals and birds.

They all seemed attracted to Beatrice in herds.

The children in Sunday School learned quite a lot

From Beatrice who blessed them whenever she taught.

The children are older with kids of their own.

Her influence lives on as older they've grown.

There's Claudette and Jocko and now Taffy too.

The dogs she had trained so they'd do tricks for you.

To the homes for the aged and many other places

She'd show them her dogs putting them through their paces.

Her budgies talked to her with scarcely a flaw.

She loved feathered friends like her mother-in-law.

But wait! For this story I'm getting ahead.

April 22, 1967 was when she wed.

She married a Hubbeard lad whose name is "Norm".

Together they'd face and overcome every storm;

Like the time in a hotel spent in Kingston town

And Beatrice and Norman were then dressing down.

A nice bubble bath would be Beatrice's delight.

So she bought the bubble bath soap for that night.

The bubble bath soap filled a bottle so stout.

Into the tub Beatrice poured it all out.

Then she turned on the water and oh, what a surprise!

A room full of bubbles is what met their eyes.

To hotel staff they did not want to confess.

They scrambled so quickly to clean up the mess.

When to heaven Beatrice's parents did leave

She had to take care of her young brother, Steve.

Then in a catastrophe Steve also died.

It is a good thing that they had God on their side.

July 15th now brings her to eighty years,

And having shared with her both laughter and tears,

From friends and family present and all of the rest,

We say, "Happy Birthday! We wish you the best!"

An Ode To Eva Mae Spenst

In Cavan township in Ontario

In a farm house in '34,

The sound of a new-born girl was heard

Behind a bedroom door.

As a little girl, they thought she'd die

With a kidney ailment bad;

But the doctor gave her a lollipop.

That made her sisters sad.

Mae wished to lick the icing spoon.

The girls said she could not.

She threw it through the window glass

And left a broken spot.

Her dad repaired the window

With two soup lids and a bolt.

It stayed that way for many years.

Don't make Mae mad; take note!

Of Judy and Wilma, Mae complained.

On gathered piles of stone.

They would not let her and Jean play.

They said, "Go get your own."

To high school two and a quarter miles

Often walk would Mae;

Unless she rode the jigger car

On the railroad tracks that day.

She went to business college.

She was always smart in school.

Then she worked for Ephgrave Insurance.

Her boss thought she was cool.

She went to Bible College.

Valedictorian she became.

They gave her a box to stand upon

To see her in her fame.

Then off to Whitehorse she did go

To help in the church up there.

As legal secretary she worked.

No effort did she spare

She got her driver's license there.

A Fiat car she bought.

To mechanic Hank she took her car

And saw him quite a lot.

They soon became an item.

She soon would change her life.

She brought him to Ontario.

They left as man and wife.

To Peace River in Alberta

They moved. Their goods they lugged

And they would start their family there

With Henry, Sheila, Doug.

From there to Edmonton they moved;

Then to Prince George, B.C.

A school, located very near

Was where the kids would be.

Then to their country home they moved.

The airport was nearby.

The children grew to adulthood

As planes above would fly.

Disliking snow and icy roads,

Mae said that they should move.

To Borden Crescent they did go.

The new home fit the groove.

From this house all the kids did go

And went their separate ways.

Then one by one they married.

This changed Mae's future days.

One day Hank started getting sick:

Heart, cancer and gall stone.

Then suddenly he passed away

And Mae was left alone.

She sold the house and trailer.

Doug bought a house so neat.

He fixed it up and for his mom

He made a basement suite.

So Mae's with Doug and Bridgette.

She's very much alive.

We all are here to celebrate

That she is seventy-five.

An Ode To George Hubbeard

On a cold December 26th

In year 1941,

A woman named Florence Hubbeard

Gave birth to a red-haired son.

They named this boy, "George Harold"

For he got his second name

From the name of his dear father

Whose first name was just the same.

He found his oldest siblings

Were young women and young men,

For he, being born the youngest,

It brought the total to ten.

He found a buddy, Austin,

Living at a farm nearby.

They shared great times together

Until Austin said, "Good-bye".

While George walked through a midway,

A woman yelled, "Hey, Red!"

George looked her way. If looks could kill

That woman would be dead.

When George began his dating,

To Port Hope he'd often go.

Returning, once, he fell asleep

And in the ditch did go.

The girl friend George did marry.

To this couple two girls came.

They filled the home with laughter,

Barb and Marilyn by name.

They got a spider monkey

That loved to scratch and bite.

It overdosed on Kathy's pills.

Oh, what a joyous night!

He worked for Ken C. Cardwell.

A backhoe he did run.

He hit one brother on the head

And half-buried the other one.

When George's marriage faltered

He was sadly left alone,

With Marilyn and Barbie,

Whom He cared for on his own.

Then Jean's friend, Betty Ephgrave,

Finally one day George did meet.

'Twas clear that he liked Betty

And she thought that he was sweet.

Soon those two started dating,

And by his heart was lead.

It wasn't too long after

That George and Betty wed.

In time they had a baby

Who's now a fine young man;

So I think that is was fitting

That they named this boy Adam.

The Causeway Pentecostal Church

Was where they would attend.

They helped in every way they could

And much time there did spend.

When Barb and Marilyn married

Then a grandpa George became.

When your children too have children

Life will never be the same.

Now in Peterborough city,

Is where George and Betty live.

We, at this celebration,

Our best wishes to George give.

An Ode To Ken C. Cardwell

My first recollection of Ken C. Cardwell,

When I was around age of four,

Was when I asked who Ken and Judy could be

Who came oft through our farmhouse door.

Mom said, "That's your sister and her husband, Ken,

Who visit us week-ends, you see."

It left me confused in my juvenile mind.

I thought sisters should live there with me.

Now Ken was a handsome man, even from his youth;

A good catch, girls knew from the start,

But Marion Ethelda was more than their match,

For she, Judy, had captured his heart.

The years passed by quickly and two sons were born

Amidst foster children galore.

Adopting a boy and two girls whom they loved,

Ken and Judy then added three more.

When I was just twelve and my dad passed away,

It was then Ken a mentor became.

He'd always worked hard so he gave me a job

And taught me to work hard the same.

After working at Raybestos for many a year,

K.C. Cardwell Construction he'd started.

Some mocked him and said that it never would work

But this did not leave Ken downhearted.

With hard work and honesty Ken did succeed

As he helped many others as well.

His faith in the Lord he held strong in his heart

And to all who would hear he would tell.

Ken had a kind heart, reaching outward to all.

He had dreams he would never fulfill,

But he left an example for others to see.

What he planted in me's with me still.

Now Ken's gone to heaven, a far better place,

And I'm sure that he'll never be bored,

For I know he's rejoicing with Jesus, his Lord,

Enjoying his heavenly reward.

Eighty Years With Wilma

Wilma Henrietta Gertrude,

Born just four score years ago;

Came to grace the Hubbeard family,

Her dad's favourite, all would know.

As a teen she'd walk to high school.

Two and a half miles seemed so far.

Sometimes she, when at the railroad,

Hitched a ride on the jigger car.

Wilma met a Maritimer,

Aubrey Densmore Smith, his name.

Soon the wedding was to happen.

Though quite sick still Aubrey came.

Steve was born and shortly after

Wilma learned to drive a car.

This would give her much more freedom.

On her own she could go far.

Wilma was a working lady

At the Bank of Montreal,

Until she gave birth to Brenda.

This event would end it all.

She loved time spent at the cottage,

In the woods at Belmont Lake.

Many times with friends and family

Happy memories they would make.

Wilma loved to make up stories,

Which to children she would tell.

They would listen with attention

And their little hearts would swell.

One was of a man so sickly,

Crying, "Dying", again and again.

A boy and girl came to his rescue.

This story we've recalled since then.

Helping Aubrey piling firewood,

A mouse ran up inside her pants.

Wilma jumped and did some yelling,

As she learned the Rodent Dance.

She loves spending time with family;

Her grand-children her delight.

She enjoys when they sleep over.

Spoiling them just seems so right.

Once a flood engulfed the basement;

Something Wilma won't forget;

The carpet inches under water

And all things were soaking wet.

Vacuuming, pumping and mopping,

Slowly dry the basement grew.

Renovations brought new carpet.

She was glad when it was through.

Wilma's had some great adventures,

Travelling all across the land.

She's seen mountains, plains and oceans,

Villages and cities grand.

Wilma's life has been fulfilling.

How the years behind have sped.

We wish good things for the future,

With the best things yet ahead.

TRUCKING

A Trucker Kind of Day

I woke up early feeling great

Before the sun did shine.

I grabbed a bite and coffee cup.

I knew things would be fine.

A little bit of snow did fall.

I drove to get my load.

I hit some ice beneath the snow

And slid across the road.

A tow truck drove by with a car

Recovered from some ditch.

I slowly drove my truck around.

I left without a hitch.

I drove more slowly now, of course,

Quite shaken by my slide.

I saw more vehicles spun 'round,

Along this icy ride.

Behind another rig I drove,

Within his tracks I stuck.

He stopped, I stopped and then a van

Behind me hit my truck.

I was not hurt nor was my truck,

But he felt very sad.

The van was smashed. Its hood was creased.

It had a damaged rad.

When all was settled I drove on.

I backed up to the dock;

I picked up all the freight for me.

I looked up at the clock.

I'd lost two hours with wasted time.

Now I was very late.

I'd not be home by supper time

If going at this rate.

The sun came out and warmed the land.

The snow began to melt.

I'd make good time now with this trip.

At least, that's how I felt.

The sky was clear. The road soon dried.

I travelled fast again.

I came up to a railroad track

And waited for a train.

Arriving at the border soon,

I parked and left my truck.

The broker said the paperwork

Was wrong so I was stuck.

With phone calls made and faxes sent

They fixed up all my stuff.

But then a cranky customs man

Said, "It's not good enough!"

Back to the broker I did go

As time sped on that day.

He got things just as customs wants;

Then I was on my way.

About ten minutes later on

A loud bang I did hear.

The engine made a funny noise

That filled my heart with fear.

I stopped the engine, parked the truck

And looked to find the cause.

The turbo pipe had blown off.

To fix it I must pause.

I called the truck shop in our town,

Though it was far away.

He said to hook it back up tight

And then go on my way.

But then this man said that I must

Keep r.p.m.'s quite low.

It meant more time to make the trip,

For now I must go slow.

I watched the cars, annoyed at me,

Fly past, then cut in front.

Some even hit their brakes real hard

And them I almost bunt.

My stomach soon began to growl.

The time had come to dine.

I saw a place with lots of trucks.

I knew the food was fine.

When I was full and paid my bill

A shock awaited me.

Graffiti covered all my truck;

An awful sight to see.

I looked and there were other trucks;

Yes, there were quite a few,

By vandals decorated as

They sat there out of view.

I went inside and told the rest

Of this deed that was done.

In anger and with disbelief

They came out on the run.

When everything had settled down

I climbed up in my truck.

Then driving from the parking lot,

Out on the road I struck.

The day dragged on, then I was stopped.

A plane had hit the road.

We had to reroute 'round the site.

'Twas slow by any mode.

One company I could not find,

Though I looked hard and long.

The address the dispatcher gave

Was absolutely wrong.

With phone calls made, directions giv'n

I found the place at last.

Eventually I carried on

With deadlines now long past.

I got back to the customs where

A friendly man, it's true,

Said that I'd have to go inside.

My PARS did not go through.

Two hours passed before a man

Said that I now was free;

But only after I had changed

My PARS to RMD.

I hurried on my way from there.

My goal was our own yard.

Then suddenly I heard a bang.

The steering wheel pulled hard.

A tire flat was now my plight.

A mobile truck repair

I called to come and fix my flat

So I could leave from there.

With wheel renewed and my cash spent

Back home I made my way.

I'd hoped for special things but got

An ordinary day.

Axles

Without the axles trucks would sit

And drivers then would walk.

I must admit that axles aren't

Of which we often talk.

However every truck which drives

The highways, as you see,

Will have two types of axles strong

And some have even three.

On trailers, trailer axles fit

Which then the tractors pull.

They must be strong to hold the load

In case the trailer's full.

All trucks have steering axles

Allowing them to steer.

They give maneuverability

To guide them far or near.

But with no power axles

The trucks just would not go.

They'd sit beside the roadside.

This fact I think you know.

Our lives too need these axles.

With one our lives we'll steer.

The other gives us power

So storms we need not fear.

The steering axle is God's Word

Which guides us every day.

For power we've the Holy Ghost,

Our power for the way.

We need them both together

For one just will not do.

They complement each other

To work in me and you.

Anointed by the Spirit

The Word works well in pow'r.

Allow them both to work and you'll

Be balanced every hour.

The Christian Trucker

He's up long before dawn.

He's a trucker.

He checks his truck and load.

Then he starts the engine.

He waits.

The air pressure must build up.

Finally all is ready.

He pulls out on to the highway.

He's rolling.

He doesn't have to wait.

He comes to the weigh scales.

He must drive in.

He lines up behind the other trucks.

He has no choice.

He waits.

Finally, he crosses the scales.

If approved, he drives on.

If not, he pulls into the parking lot.

He gathers up the papers and goes inside.

He waits.

If it's inspection time, he really waits.

Finally, he's on the road again.

Traffic jam ahead!

He waits.

At last he moves through the heavy traffic.

He drives on.

He pulls up to the docks to be unloaded.

The forklift is out of propane.

He waits.

Finally the unloading is done.

Now he has goods to load.

Paperwork has to be completed.

Some freight is not ready yet.

He waits.

Finally everything is finished.

The freight is loaded.

With paperwork completed he drives on.

He comes to another weigh scales.

Another wait!

Finally, he's back on the highway.

The engine rumbles.

The tires hum.

This is the trucker's motivation.

No waiting now.

All too soon he's at the border.

The trucks are backed up.

He must pull behind the last truck.

He joins the lineup.

He waits.

Finally, he gets to park in the parking lot.

He must go into customs.

Then he can go to see the broker.

At the broker's they process his paperwork.

He waits.

With the paperwork done he walks to his truck.

He lines up behind other trucks.

He still is in a lineup.

He has to report to the border guard.

He waits.

Finally, he gets to the booth.

Because he has too many manifests

He has to park and go into customs.

He puts his papers in the rack.

He waits.

Finally, a customs officer picks up his papers

They are processed; All but one set.

It's not in the computer system!

Lost somewhere in cyberspace somewhere, I suppose.

He waits.

The officer still cannot find the set of papers.

It simply can't be found.

It's looking for the internet path to customs.

Maybe the pathway sign reads,

Www.customs.wait .

He keeps waiting.

At least he gets to meet trucker friends.

They're waiting too.

Finally, the paperwork clears, but,

He has met friends because he waits.

Now he's on his way.

A BMW cuts him off,

Then brakes in front of him to miss the traffic ahead.

He brakes hard to avoid the traffic snarl.

He waits.

He's used to it.

Owners of expensive cars or 4x4's

Seem to think they're invincible.

He knows better.

They should learn to wait.

He's seen BMW accordions before.

He remembers, "pray for those who spitefully use you."

He prays for the driver's safety and salvation.

Traffic starts to pick up speed.

No longer does he wait.

A pickup zips past, blowing his horn.

The driver makes obscene hand motions.

The driver mouths expletive deletives.

The driver doesn't like slow trucks.

The driver doesn't like to wait.

He ignores the nonsense.

He's used to it.

He continues on,

Wheeling down the highway now.

He wishes others could wait like he does.

Enjoying every moment.

Suddenly a woman in a car to his left accelerates.

She swerves in front, narrowly missing the truck's fender.

She nails the brake and then cuts to the exit ramp on

the right.

I guess she could not wait.

He brakes hard.

This time he pulls the air horn cord.

He's tired of this kind of thing.

He's also a bit shaken.

He waits to calm down.

He suddenly remembers:

"Bless and curse not."

He asks God to forgive him.

He prays for her good.

He prays that she'll learn to wait.

He turns off the highway.

He enters the town where he is headed.

Oh, oh, flashing red lights ahead!

The barricades are down.

He's going to have to wait.

A train is coming somewhere.

Oh, there it is way down the track.

It's coming very slowly.

It takes what seems a long time.

He waits.

At last the traffic moves on.

Finally, he reaches his destination.

The forklift operator is on coffee break.

He won't get unloaded soon.

He waits.

He reads the Word.

He writes down some thoughts.

Soon he'll be unloaded.

He'll pick up another load.

He uses up time as he waits.

He'll work his way through heavy traffic,

Stopping again for weigh scales and customs.

Finally he'll be on his way.

With the long day past he's finally home.

He won't have to wait.

At home his wife will greet him.

She'll ask, "anything special happen today?"

He'll reply, "no, just the ordinary."

This Christian trucker just wants a shower,

But, for details she'll just have to wait.

The Trucker

The trucker rises while it's dark

Before the sun is up.

He checks his load. He checks his truck

And possibly a pup.

He checks the levels, tires and brakes.

He checks the wheel lugs too.

He checks all systems to be sure

They'll do what they should do.

He starts the engine, lets it warm

And checks the gauges bright.

The driver log book he fills out,

Then checks out every light.

With all things checked and verified

And happy with his load,

Then he's allowed to shift in gear

To move out on the road.

Then rolling, rolling on he goes.

The highway he does take.

A long day lies ahead for him.

His schedule he must make.

Through stormy weather all around;

Through hail, rain, wind or calm,

The trucks keep moving through the land,

The goods transported on.

The truckers keep our country well,

Delivering what it needs;

A strong economy to maintain

So on the trucker speeds.

Lonely at times is the trucker's life

As he drives on alone.

He feels the loss of family time

Because it's too soon gone.

We need good truckers in our land.

They do a job well done.

They work real hard to bring their loads

And so they make their run.

When truckers on the road you see

Be sure to give them room.

Don't cut them off or tailgate close

Or it could be your doom.

The truckers in this land, my friend,

When all is said and done,

Are making life real good for you

And things so smoothly run.

Hats off to all the men and women

Behind the steering wheel

Who carry shipments far and wide!

Their contribution's real.

TRUCK SIGNS

A tractor-trailer had two signs

That brought to me delight,

With "EL PASSO" written on the left;

"EL CRUNCHO" on the right.

If you don't see the humour there,

Trucks you don't know, no doubt.

You need a safety driving course

To see what it's about.

Another truck, the Milky Way,

That pulls a silver pup,

Has signs behind and on both sides

Which always cheer me up.

The first says "FRESH FROM FARM TO YOU",

There on the tank so fine.

The second confidently says,

"MILK TASTES GREAT ANYTIME".

A happy cow smiles back as well.

The third is quite a spiel.

If you can, try to say it fast:

"DRINKAMUGAMILKAMEAL".

A driver drove a fancy rig.

His sign was meant to please us.

He drove like the devil, as they say,

But it said, "TRUCKING FOR JESUS".

His name, it must have been Jehu,

Like the man found in God's Word,

Who drove his rig quite furiously

Saying it was for the Lord.

In ways we all are like these trucks.

Folks read our lives each day.

I wonder what they're finding there.

Friend what does your life say?

Why Go Trucking?

Most truckers talk about their jobs,

Complaining as they go.

Their companies are just not fair

And everyone should know.

The dispatcher is such a jerk.

The boss is one big twit

And drivers are the only ones

Whose actions all are fit.

The diesel costs are way too high.

The income is too low.

The breakdowns come too frequently.

Too many tires blow.

So on and on the list will go

Of problems which they spout.

You wonder if these problems are

Just things to talk about.

Why, then, would truckers want to drive

With problems, rain and mud?

Just ask them and they all will say,

It's simply in their blood.

WHEN IT HURTS

Almost Overcome

I pour my heart out to you, Lord.

I hope you'll hear my plea.

Though right now far away you seem

I fall on bended knee.

My situation crushes me.

It's getting hard to take.

If things continue as they are

I'm sure I soon will break.

Yet silently I suffer on

And things seem so unfair

The longed for change seems far away.

The pain is hard to bear.

My faith is quickly vanishing.

All hope seems far away.

With hope deferred the heart gets sick.

I'm nauseous today.

If this is what You've planned for me,

Your will brought grief and pain;

But if I read Your Scriptures right

The end result is gain.

First Peter one and nineteen says

That we all might have grief,

But it is good and in due time

The Lord will bring relief.

So I will strive to carry on

And try to do my best

While trusting God to see me through

And bring me into rest.

Cliches

A heart is pained.

She suffers all alone.

One tells her, "It's okay."

"God still is on His throne."

"It's not okay!"

She cries and she is right.

She wants this God to come

And brighten up her night.

A broken heart

Grieves from committed wrong.

"You reap just what you sow,"

One says and moves along.

He knows he's wrong.

He needs no cliché curt.

He needs someone to care

And see him through his hurt.

Cliches will not resolve

The problems in this life.

They just increase the pain

That comes from sin and strife.

Cliches hold truth,

But they weren't meant to heal.

Compassion from a loving heart

Is what folks need to feel.

They may sound cute,

Yet wisdom does not reign

Within those flippant words,

Which bring so little gain.

Such empty words!

Let's leave them far behind.

The words that bring real hope

With healing let us find.

Defeating Depression

When facing deep depression

A doctor you should see,

So he can then determine

Just what the cause might be.

If no cause medical he finds

For why you're feeling blue,

But it is circumstantial,

There are things you can do.

Don't run away from others

And hide up on the shelf,

But do a deed of kindness.

You'll find good 'bout yourself.

Then note one's sad condition

That's far worse than your own.

Give thanks to God for favour

That He to you has shown.

Seek someone who's discouraged.

Who's feeling sad and down.

Speak hope, encouragement and love.

Help take away the frown.

Read from the Holy Scriptures,

Sent to us from above,

About how God does care for you

And bathe in God's great love.

Go walk in God's creation.

See what the Lord has done.

In awe observe the beauty,

Revealed to everyone.

To children facing boredom

A happy story tell.

Observe the wonder in their eyes,

As all things turn out well.

Tune in to joyful worship

And let it lift your soul.

Join in with your own praises.

It helps to make you whole.

Sit down and write a letter

To some friends far away.

Encourage them with goodness

To brighten up their day.

Observe a needy person,

Whose hunger brings him pain.

Buy him a lunch without a charge

And bring him hope again.

Give God great adoration

And praise because He's God.

Just knowing He is worthy

As your own soul is awed.

Each thing that fades depression

Removes self off your mind,

To think on something different

Real peace and joy to find.

Dormant Time

Sometimes in life when things go flat

And God seems far away,

You wonder if God doesn't care

Or if you've gone astray.

It may be it's a special time

That comes to make you grow.

Although it seems the opposite,

There's something you should know.

A dormant time will often come

When we have felt great pain.

It seems that God has walked away,

But this is for our gain.

The Word says we are branches fair

And Jesus is the vine.

Sometimes God has some pruning done

To keep our lives in line.

He does not want to bring us hurt

But prune us back must He.

He takes some things out of our lives

To make us fruitful be.

The gard'ner prunes his vines each year

When fall has taken hold.

The vine goes into dormancy

To face the winter's cold.

It's no mistake, the way it's done.

It's our Creator's plan.

When pruned by God, don't be surprised

That waiting comes to man.

The vine in winter looks quite dead:

Cut back, no leaves, so sad.

There seems to be no hope at all.

To us its fate seems bad.

It seems that dormancy goes on

And it will never end.

Then comes a stirring deep inside.

Spring's just around the bend.

The pruning of our God does hurt.

The dormancy seems long.

However, spring is drawing near

And brings with it a song.

When everything seems over then

And bleakness fills each day,

Remember spring that brings new life

Will soon be on its way.

With winter gone, new warmth will come.

A freshness you will know.

Leaves will spring forth and blossoms flower.

Then brand new fruit will grow

As sure as pruning must be done

And winter follows fall,

The dormancy that you have known

Is worth it after all.

Falsely Accused

My heart was broken from the blow:

Accused for that which was not true.

My innocence I could not prove

And there was nothing I could do.

Someone had seen and heard me once.

Not knowing all, she soon was gone.

Based on a partial truth she spoke

Assuming wrong that was not done.

She shared the rumour with her friends.

The lie, believed, spread all the more.

When surfacing in all its shame,

It slashed me down and left me sore.

My reputation by these words

Was ruined, crushed and left to die.

With no defense allowed, I fell;

Destroyed by someone's twisted lie.

I asked the Lord about this thing.

In innocence I asked him, "Why?"

Accused by people, thought my friends,

In pain I wanted just to die.

Then God brought memories of His Son,

Who came to face great pain and strife.

Falsely accused, He bore the shame

And by it giving up His life.

He understands for He does know

How falsehoods hurt and tear the soul.

Jesus, alone, can heal the wounds,

Restoring one to make him whole.

When one's accused by someone's lies,

To say he's blessed somehow seems wrong;

But in His Word God says it's true

And he will finally come out strong.

When falsehoods are against you flung

And you're condemned, though they're not true,

Turn to the One who understands.

He'll give you love and bring you through.

Grace In Suffering

I believe God spoke to me.

I was shocked as I could be.

"Suffering is a gift of grace.

God's love brings trials that you face."

"Grace" means "favour from our Lord";

It's recorded in God's Word.

Grace and suffering do not seem

To link together as a team.

It's difficult to understand

How suff'rings that I have to bear

With glories in eternity

Prepared for me cannot compare.

But God knows what is best for me

For he can see what I can't see.

He sends those things which ought to be

Since he plans for eternity.

Although it's hard to trust in God

And walk with confidence in Him,

I must believe the Lord will bring

The very best when hope is dim.

How Can I Praise When I Feel This Way?

"In everything give thanks" and "Rejoice forevermore"?

Yes, they seem such easy things to do, it's true.

Yet when I am inundated by the trials of this life,

I find that they're very difficult to do.

When everything is fine and the sun's rays shine so bright

We are filled with thankfulness and joyous song.

When our lives turn topsy-turvy and the outlook's

looking dark,

We feel sadness and for better days we long.

In great sorrow and afflictions when God's presence you

can't sense;

Then abandoned and alone is how you feel.

Just remember God still loves you and is walking by

your side.

He'll go with you for His care for you is real.

You cannot live by feelings for they surely will deceive.

There are times that you won't feel God's love, so free.

Lift your eyes by faith to Jesus, as you trust Him with your life.

Just rejoice with thanks for things that are to be.

Loneliness

A housewife's busy all the day,

With little children in the way.

She cooks, she cleans, she irons away,

But feels the pangs of loneliness.

A pastor with a hearty laugh

Serves faithfully with his large staff.

Of his work folks don't know the half.

He feels the grip of loneliness.

A trucker driving down the road

Takes pains in hauling every load,

But in his heart deep things are stowed.

He often aches with loneliness.

A single woman by herself

Feels somehow left up on the shelf.

She thinks there's little worth in self.

She often cries with loneliness.

A leader in his field awakes

And finds that he has made mistakes.

The loss of job and friends he takes.

Depression comes with loneliness.

A young man with a scraggly beard

Is labeled "strange" and even "weird".

No friends for him have e'er appeared.

He lives a life of loneliness.

Regarding neither tongue nor race,

No matter what the class or face,

It finds in hearts a certain place.

This thing which we call loneliness.

There is a friend for you and me

Who once died on a rugged tree,

Saying, "why have you forsaken me?"

He understands our loneliness.

This Jesus wants to be your friend.

He's one on whom you can depend.

He'll with you loving moments spend.

He'll help to ease your loneliness.

Loser

Loser, loser, loser!"
That's what they all did say.
"You'll always be a loser
'Til you face your dying day."

Reacting in defiance
I rose above the throng.
I would succeed and show them
That all of them were wrong.

I did advance with all my might.
I felt I had success.
I overcame and where I'd come
Nobody had to guess.

Then in the midst of vict'ry
My world fell all apart.
It broke in tiny pieces.
I nursed a broken heart.

The friends I had all left me.

An arrow pierced my soul.

My spirit now was shattered,

My life an empty hole.

I sat among the pieces.

My heart was filled with fears.

The cry, "You are a loser!"

Came ringing in my ears.

Where were the Christian people

Who lift the wounded souls?

I only felt depression

With empty unreached goals.

The word says, "more than conquerors"

And "victory through our Lord".

How can I triumph this way

According to God's Word?

The answer comes quite gently.

God knows we are as grass.

He knows our human failures.

These things shall surely pass.

My emptiness the Lord sees.

He feels my grief and pain.

Because he cares, He'll heal me

And pick me up again.

Self-confidence had vanished

For doing any thing,

But I know I can do all things

Through Jesus Christ the king.

"A winner", Jesus calls me.

A loser I can't be,

For I am teamed with Jesus

Now and through eternity

Mad At God

"I'm mad at God", you'd like to say?

It seems He isn't fair?

You've suffered through the fire's heat?

It's time your beefs to air?

God at us must in sadness look.

He knows you've suffered pain.

Afflictions that have come to you

God saw descend like rain.

God takes no joy in watching you

Face ridicule and loss.

Your bitterness let God remove.

Just leave it at the cross.

Why does our God not something do

And stop these evil ones,

Who bring such loss, scorn, hurt and shame

To His daughters and His sons?

If God would quickly judge these ones,

In order to be fair,

He'd have to judge us all as well.

Of hurts we've brought our share.

We've all brought pain to others' lives,

Intended or maybe not.

No human here is innocent

From this sin's awful blot.

The only One whose life was clean,

Hung suffering 'til dead,

Receiving judgment for our wrongs.

He suffered in our stead.

Our sufferings of heat and fire,

And waters bleak and cold,

Refine us if we yield to God.

Then we come forth as gold.

God won't remove all trials of life,

But for us will be there.

He won't allow our trials to be

More than each one can bear.

He'll take your hand. He'll carry you,

Though you can't sense Him there.

Just take His hand. He'll lead you through,

A smile again to wear.

Mired

I'm stuck in the mire of failure,

Bogged down in the guck and the goo.

I've messed up so badly all things have gone wrong.

There's nothing that I know to do.

I tried to do that which was proper.

Instead I did little but fail.

I hurt those to whom I should have brought joy.

I guess that I did nothing well.

My friends that I trusted have left me,

And now I am stuck all alone.

I call out to God, but the heavens seem brass.

My heart seems as cold as a stone.

Religious folks pass on the pathway.

But I know that they really don't care.

They sneer or they mock as they go 'cross the road

And on they go leaving me there.

But some of them stop by the wayside

And try to push me even deeper,

While some of them dig at the road's sloping banks

To make the climb up even steeper.

I don't need to hear more pat answers.

Advice to get out does not bless.

I need to have someone to reach down a hand

And pull me up out of this mess.

I look up and I find my answer.

God promised and will if I wait.

Although it is hard to keep waiting some more,

I know the Lord never is late.

It's not by a perfect performance

On which our dear Lord God does base

His wonderful mercy, His blessing and love.

They simply come by His free grace.

So I will just call to the Saviour

And ask that He soon bring me out.

I'll trust and believe for He said that He would.

I'll determine to squash every doubt.

The Dark Tunnel

Sometimes it seems you're all alone

And no-one understands.

All friends you've had are far away

In far-off distant lands.

You wonder if the Lord above

Had too abandoned you;

Although his Word has promised that

He always will be true.

You think, "Is this a punishment

For having done some wrong?"

Yet you can't understand it for

You've served God all along.

You must know it's not punishment

For wrong things done by you.

It is a tunnel God has giv'n;

A place you must go through.

The tunnel is so difficult

Because it's just like night.

But there is hope. You'll soon be through

Into the brightest light.

Your tunnel seems to never stop,

As right, then left it wends.

Then as you round this final curve

You find the tunnel ends.

Don't try to comprehend God's plan

While traveling in this way.

He soon will guide you onward to

Enjoy the light of day.

Then you will find a time to heal

As you recuperate.

You'll gain the power to bless and help

Those in a broken state.

The reason for this test from God

You may not understand;

But God will use it as he leads

Into a fruitful land.

When through some tunnels folks must walk

And find it hard to stand,

They'll find in you a healing balm

Because you understand.

The Nail

At times in life when beaten down

I've felt much like a nail.

If it could talk I'd like to know

The nature of its tale.

The hammer, no doubt, would be viewed

As that nail's greatest foe.

The hammer's purpose is to pound

The nail, to make it go.

The nail's self-image would be bad.

Its purpose is quite plain.

It just exists to get its head

Struck hard and then again.

The hammer, though, is not the foe.

It's in the craftsman's hand,

Who holds the nail and then decides

Just where the tool must land.

The hammer, then, will pound the nail

And maybe its point clinch.

The workman fastens tight the wood.

To him it is a cinch.

The nail is often out of sight.

No more will it be seen.

It does its job but no-one notes,

As if it had not been.

The nail, in order to be used,

On it some blows must land,

But like the hammer it is held

Within the master's hand.

Sometimes when blows upon you fall

And difficult is life,

It seems that all you ever see

Are trials, pain and strife.

You feel like you are beaten down.

You feel just like the nail.

Know you're still in the Master's hand

And His love will not fail.

You may feel small and out of sight.

No purpose you discern,

But that you're holding things in place

You too some day may learn.

When you are thinking things are tough

And that life isn't fair,

Remember God still holds you tight

And truly He does care.

TWO POEMS BY MY DAUGHER, CYNTHIA STATHAM

Drayton Valley Christmas

December 2014

'Twas the night before Christmas

And all through the town

The hotels were empty

Not a rigger was found

The streets were so quiet

Few pickups to see

Not a Ford or a Dodge

But few GMCs

Only families were left

Celebrating the season

The fun had begun

And we all know the reason

With a glance down 50th

To the left and the right

It's time to tuck in

For this Christmas Eve night

To the sounds of the pump jacks

And sounds of the mill

May your Christmas bring you

A joy and a thrill

What is Faith

October 23,1999

A little bit of hope

Comes my way

A load of doubt

Takes it away

For every good thing

That I see

Something so bad

Is blinding me

What do I pray for

Do I dare

Worry assails me

Gives me a scare

Say I do pray

And nothing appears

What is faith

Amidst my fears

So I make the choice

Again I pray

God send a miracle

Out my way

What is faith

Amidst my fears

It's trying again

Through all the tears

Proof

Made in the USA
Charleston, SC
25 September 2015